Developing Standards-based Assessment Tasks
for English as a First Foreign Language

André A. Rupp, Miriam Vock,
Claudia Harsch & Olaf Köller

Developing Standards-based Assessment Tasks for English as a First Foreign Language

Context, Processes, and Outcomes in Germany

In collaboration with:
Rita Green, Michael Leucht, Daniela Neumann,
Raphaela Oehler, Hans-Anand Pant,
Henning Rossa & Konrad Schröder

Volume 1

Waxmann 2008
Münster / New York / München / Berlin

Bibliographic information published by the Deutsche Nationalbibliothek
The Deutsche Nationalbibliothek lists this publication in the
Deutsche Nationalbibliografie; detailed bibliographic data are
available in the Internet at http://dnb.d-nb.de.

ISBN 978-3-8309-1943-8

© Waxmann Verlag GmbH, Münster 2008

www.waxmann.com
info@waxmann.com

Cover design: Christian Averbeck, Münster
Layout: Stoddart Satz- und Layoutservice, Münster
Print: Hubert & Co., Göttingen

Printed on age-resistant paper,
acid-free as per ISO 9706

All rights reserved
Printed in Germany

Table of Contents

Preamble 7

Section I – Political and Historical Context 9
The Role of International Student Assessments 11
Plans for Educational Reform in Germany 12
The Conception of the National Educational Standards 13
Standards-based Quality Assurance through the Institute for Educational Progress 15

Section II – Foundations for Test Development 19
The Common European Framework of Reference for Languages 21
    Political Objectives of the CEF 21
    The Language Model of the CEF 22
    Scales and Competence Levels in the CEF 23
    Consequences for the Use of the CEF in Schools 24
National Educational Standards for a First Foreign Language (English/French) 25
    Competency Areas and Individual Competencies in the NES 26
    Consequences for the Development of Standards-based Tests 28

Section III – English Language Learning in Germany 31
The Role of English Internationally 33
The Role of English in Germany 34
Differences in First, Second, and Foreign Language Acquisition 37
Implications for the Development of Standards-based Tests 38

Section IV – Test Specifications 41
Synopsis 43
Test Purpose 44
    Resulting Proficiency Scales 44
    Resulting Decisions about Students 45
Other Tests Linked to the CEF 45
    The Cambridge ESOL Exams 46
    The TOEFL 47
    The DIALANG System 48
    The Trinity College GESE and ISE Exams 49
    The Tests of the DESI Study 51

Section V – Construct Definitions 53
Reading Comprehension 55
    The Assessment of Reading Comprehension in Large-scale Assessments 55
    The Description of Reading Comprehension in the NES and the CEF 57
    The Construct Definition in the Research Literature 57
    The Construct Definition in the DESI Study 61
    The Construct Definition for the Tests Developed at the IQB 62

    Listening Comprehension 64
        The Assessment of Listening Comprehension in Large-scale Assessments 64
        The Description of Listening Comprehension in the NES and the CEF 65
        The Construct Definition in the Research Literature.. 66
        The Construct Definition in the DESI Study 67
        The Construct Definition for the Tests Developed at the IQB 69
    Writing 71
        The Assessment of Writing in Large-scale Assessments 71
        The Description of Writing in the NES and the CEF 72
        The Construct Definition in the Research Literature.. 73
        The Construct Definition in the DESI Study 75
        The Construct Definition for the Tests Developed at the IQB 76

Section VI – Overview of the Item and Task Development Process................................ 79
Structure of Item and Task Development Process 81
Composition of Expert Group 85
Profile of Trainer and Workshops 86

Section VII – Preliminary Empirical Investigations of Items and Tasks......................... 87
Pre-trials of Reading and Listening Comprehension Tasks... 89
Extra Trials of Reading and Listening Comprehension Tasks.. 89
Pre-trial of Writing Tasks.. 92
Extra Trial of Writing tasks... 93
Feasibility Study of Writing Tasks 96

Section VIII – Characteristics of Tasks in the Field Trial Pool 99
Characteristics of Reading Comprehension Tasks... 101
Characteristics of Listening Comprehension Tasks... 105
Characteristics of Writing Tasks... 109

References 113

Appendices 123
Thematic Glossary... 125
Appendix A: Sample Grids from CEF 130
Appendix B: National Educational Standards for English
                     as a First Foreign Language 135
Appendix C: Construct Definitions in the CEF, the NES,
                     and other Large-scale Assessments.. 149
Appendix D: Rating Scales for Writing Tasks 156
Appendix E: Information on Item Development... 165
Appendix F: Dutch Grid Classification Criteria for Reading
                     and Listening Tasks... 172
Appendix G: Standardized Feedback Questionnaires for Pre-trials 175

Authors.. 183

Preamble

This document is the first in a multi-part technical report series that describes the development, calibration, and validation of standards-based tests for English as a first foreign language at the *Institute for Educational Progress (Institut zur Qualitätsentwicklung im Bildungswesen, IQB)* in Berlin, Germany. The entire report series can be viewed as the documentary cornerstone that provides evidence for what Bachman (2005) calls the *assessment use argument* for these tests, which is comprised of the *assessment validity argument* and the *assessment utilization argument*. This first report lays the theoretical and empirical foundations for this argument and describes preliminary pieces of evidence for different elements within such arguments. Its objective is to provide a transparent description of the item development process that illustrates the numerous decisions that were made during this process to make overt the resulting consequences for interpreting scores from the standards-based tests as well as the decisions that could be based on these interpretations.

This report describes the process of item development in alignment with the *National Educational Standards (NES)* (i.e., the *Länderübergreifende Bildungsstandards*) for English as a first foreign language at the upper secondary level for the *Hauptschulabschluss* (KMK, 2004) and the *Mittlerer Schulabschluss* (KMK, 2004) and is divided into eight main sections. In the first section, historical background information about the context within which the NES were formulated and the IQB was created is provided. In the second section, the primary theoretical frameworks for the test development process are provided, which are the NES for English as a first foreign language and the *Common European Framework of Reference for Languages (CEF)* (Council of Europe, 2001). In the third section, a portrayal of the role of English as a first foreign language for German students is developed and differences between first, second, and foreign language acquisition are outlined. In the fourth section, the specifications of the standards-based tests including a description of their purpose and the decisions that are made with them about learners are described. Furthermore, other current tests for English as a second or foreign language that are linked to the CEF are reviewed. In the fifth section, detailed descriptions of the constructs that the tests are attempting to measure are given based on reviews of the research literature on the constructs and the operationalization of these constructs in other large-scale assessment studies. In the sixth section, the process of item development is described in detail including the selection and training of item writers and the process of item sharing and item review. In the seventh section, key results from various pre- and extra-trials that were conducted to obtain preliminary empirical evidence for the functioning of the items are presented. In the eighth and final section, the item pool that was developed by the item writers on the basis of these construct definitions and the theoretical frameworks in which they are grounded is characterized. This is followed by complete references for all sections as well as an extensive appendix with additional reference information that is referred to in the text. The report is written for a non-technical audience; thus, all key terms are defined, explained, and collected in a glossary at the end of the report.

This first report in the technical report series does not describe the planning, implementation, analysis, or reporting strategies for the field and main trials, which are the main empirical sources of evidence for the establishment of the proficiency scales and the interpretations and decisions based on them. Nor does it describe the process of standard-setting that is used to establish cut-scores for the resulting scales. This information will be contained in future reports in the technical report series, which will be available starting with the summer of 2009. These reports will be written after the completion of these processes and associated research studies. The publication of these reports as well as that of research papers on related topics will be announced on the website of the IQB (http://www.iqb.hu-berlin.de).

This report reflects the joint efforts of a large number of collaborators that were instrumental in the planning, implementation, and documentation of the work conducted in this project. We would like to thank particularly all the teachers from the federal states, who spent many hours developing test items and classroom tasks, and who attended nine week-long sessions of professional development outside their regular teaching loads. We would also like to thank Dr. Rita Green for her comprehensive training during the item development process as well as Dr. Neus Figueras, Dr. Felianka Kaftandjieva, Dr. Gabriele Kecker, Dr. Eli Moe, Prof. Dr. Dr. Rainer Lehmann, Prof. Dr. Günther Nold, and Prof. Dr. Konrad Schröder for their expert advice during regular expert meetings and outside of those. Similarly, we want to gratefully emphasize the input and dedication of Dr. Claudia Harsch and Henning Rossa, who attended many regional group meetings and built an indispensable bridge between the IQB and the item developers in the process.

We would also like to thank the doctoral students Raphaela Oehler and Michael Leucht for their commitment and dedication to this process and their continual help when deadlines got tight. We also want to explicitly recognize the many student workers, in particular Sandra Franke, who mastered the logistics of this complex project and helped with numerous aspects of the field work. Related to this, we want to acknowledge the collaboration with the *Data Processing Center* in Hamburg, especially Heiko Sibberns, Guido Martin, and Steffen Knoll who were responsible for the logistics of data collection, entry, and cleaning. They were also instrumental in helping to plan and conduct the workshop for training the raters of the writing tasks, in recruiting the raters, and in entering the data for preliminary analyses. Finally, we want to mention that there were many colleagues inside and outside the IQB who provided guidance, insight, and constructive criticism to this project; without their help, this task would not have been accomplished so swiftly and thoroughly.

Section I:
Political and Historical Context

In order to understand the meaning of *National Educational Standards (NES)* for the German education system – and, hence, the relevance of the efforts described in this report in developing tests in accordance with the standards – it is necessary to delineate how the NES evolved in the context of international student assessments for systems-monitoring and accountability purposes. For a description of the theoretical foundations of national and international large-scale student assessments and for descriptions of how results from them can be reported effectively we refer, for example, to Hosenfeld, Ophoff, and Bittins (2006).

The Role of International Student Assessments

In contrast to other countries, outcomes of school education processes had not been systematically examined in Germany before the 1990s. Instead, the main focus had been on the development and revision of detailed curricula and lesson plans that resulted in guidelines for effective instruction (i.e., an *input* orientation of schooling). Starting in the second half of the 1990s, however, a public interest in whether classroom teaching is actually successful in terms of learner achievements had emerged (i.e., an *output* orientation of schooling). These developments were motivated, in part, by the unexpectedly weak performance of German secondary students in the *Third International Mathematics and Science Study (TIMSS)* in 1997 (e.g., Baumert, Bos, & Lehmann, 2001), which measured the basic knowledge of 15 year olds in mathematics and the natural sciences.

As a consequence of the intense public debate surrounding these results, the Standing Conference of the Ministers of Education and Cultural Affairs of the Federal States in Germany (KMK) decided in its Konstanzer Beschluss in 1997 (http://www.kmk.org/aktuell/pm971024.htm) that Germany should join a host of other countries and participate on a long-term basis in international student assessments. Furthermore, it was decided that there should be complementary student assessments in Germany with random representative student samples of around 40,000 students, which are much larger than the typical international student assessment samples that consist merely of about 6,000 students. The motivation for these so-called extension studies is to obtain reliable information on the level of achievement in each federal state.

Furthermore, in the year 2000 Germany participated in the *Programme for International Student Assessment (PISA)* (e.g., Baumert et al., 2001; Prenzel et al., 2004) for the first time and has been participating in PISA ever since. PISA assesses student achievement in the areas of reading comprehension, mathematical ability and basic knowledge of the natural sciences, whereby the main focus – as reflected in the relative breadth of content coverage and number of test items employed across domains – changes across assessment cycles. The main focus of the 2000 study was on reading comprehension, whereas mathematical ability was the main focus of the 2003 cycle and basic knowledge of the natural sciences was the main focus of the 2006 cycle; these cycles will continue to be repeated every three years. Akin to TIMSS, the findings from PISA 2000 showed that German students had only achieved mediocre results, an outcome that was referred to in the press and by the general public as the so-called "PISA-shock". Moreover, the distribution of ability was extremely wide and there was a large proportion of students who performed either at the lowest competency level or even below that (e.g., Baumert et al., 2001). In addition, the study revealed a whole gamut of social and ethnic disparities within the German education system. The disadvantages suffered by students from underprivileged social strata, especially those with low socio-economic power and a migrant background, were striking and policy makers felt that steps needed to be taken to counteract this situation. One step that was taken to exclude the possibility that the poor performance of German students might be due to method effects in PISA was to conduct extension studies for PISA. The objective was to investigate whether test forms that were designed in closer agreement with German curricula would lead to superior performance of German students. The hypothesis of a test effect due to curricular alignment could, however, not be supported in general.

The participation in international student assessments and the comparison between the federal states through extension studies was recognized by policy-makers as a key empirical piece of information for system monitoring and accountability research in Germany. Therefore, in the *Plöner Beschlüsse* from June 2006 (www.kmk.org/aktuell/314_KMK_top_9_Anlage.pdf), the KMK agreed on the participation in future assessment cycles of TIMSS, PISA, and PIRLS / IGLU (e.g., Bos et al., 2003) as well as on additional comparison studies between federal states starting in 2009 onward until 2019. Of particular significance for the work described in this report is the fact that the KMK decided that the extension studies should be conducted with the test items from the standards-based assessments developed by the IQB.

Plans for Educational Reform in Germany

The results of the PISA 2000 study also rekindled an intense debate about the content of school curricula. The KMK demanded that the lessons learnt from this exercise needed to be put to good use and that an outcome-orientated learning and teaching environment needed to be fostered nationally. It was decided that only a teaching approach that promotes the development of competencies that are based on real-life demands in authentic contexts, coupled with the teaching of basic foundational skills, will achieve the long-term goal of improving the situation of education in general (see www.kmk.org/aktuell/pm011204.htm). These essential fields of action were identified by the KMK:
- increased support for students with learning difficulties,
- improvement of classroom based quality development and quality assurance,
- timely identification of 'poor readers',

- revision of the structure of the educational system, specifically with respect to school-leaving certificates and the paths that lead to them,
- more intensive use of learning periods and of learning opportunities, and
- development of improved structures for staffing and school organization.

These goals demonstrate that it was seen as paramount to uphold educational opportunities for all students independent of their personal background by supporting every student effectively in the classroom. Thus, the aim of the KMK is to improve the quality of schooling altogether, to make diverse school-leaving certificates comparable, and to achieve a general permeability of the education system within Germany (see Cortina et al., 2003, for a report on the structure of the German school system at the turn of the century). For this purpose, NES were seen as an important steering instrument, because they represent binding conventions for educational output (http://www.kmk.org/aktuell/pm020524.htm).

The Conception of the National Educational Standards

International large-scale student assessments such as TIMSS, PISA, and PIRLS / IGLU undoubtedly provided the political motivation for changes to the German education system. To ground the development of the NES not just in the theoretical frameworks of these studies but in internationally accepted theoretical frameworks for the development of standards-based assessments, a white paper commissioned on behalf of the *Federal Ministry of Education and Research (Bundesministerium für Bildung und Forschung)* and the KMK by Klieme et al. (2003) was published. It formed an important basis for the development of the NES as it outlined characteristics that the NES should have as well as conditions for and implications of their implementation. On the basis of the theoretical recommendations drawn up by the authors of the paper, the KMK agreed on NES for the *Mittlerer Schulabschluss* in German, mathematics, and the first foreign language (English/French) in December 2003. The KMK supplemented these standards in October 2004 by introducing NES for the *Mittlerer Schulabschluss* in chemistry, physics, and biology, NES for the *Hauptschulabschluss* in German, mathematics, and a first foreign language (English/ French), as well as NES for the *Primarbereich* (i.e., primary level) in German and mathematics (http://www.kmk.org/schul/home1.htm). These standards were implemented in all the federal states at the beginning of the school years starting 2004/05 or 2005/06 and are binding for each state.

The NES describe *competencies* which the students must have acquired at a certain grade level for a certain school-leaving qualification. Formally, the NES are normative structural guidelines for monitoring education systems that need to be translated into empirical models that can provide information about cross-sectional achievement status as well as longitudinal achievement trends (see Schecker & Parchmann, in press). That is, they reflect managerialist principles of governance within a neo-liberal management of education that is tied to accountability (e.g., McKay, 2005). From an international perspective, the term 'standard' can relate to different aspects such as the content, conditions, or results of teaching and learning processes.

One typically distinguishes between (a) content standards and (b) performance standards. The focus of *content standards* is on the content of learning and instruction as they describe precisely which areas of content should be taught and, most importantly, which competencies students should have acquired at a particular time point in their school career. In contrast, *performance standards* describe at what level the students need to perform to demonstrate a certain degree of achievement of the content standards as reflected in labels for different competency levels (e.g., basic, proficient, advanced; see Cizek, Bunch, & Koons, 2004). Since the competency descriptions in content and performance standards implicitly reflect policy decisions, one also distinguishes between whether ministry-set standards represent minimal, typical, or maximal expectations of student achievement. Since the NES of the KMK stipulate which competencies need to be acquired as well as the level at which they need to be acquired, they are a blend of content and performance standards. Furthermore, policy-makers have decided that they should reflect the typical achievement of the students.

In spite of their normative character, the NES are not supposed to limit the teachers in their instruction and assessment of students. Rather, they were developed with the intention to enable the development of a teaching culture that explicitly recognizes and accounts for the varying abilities of the students. Rather than being the sole prescriptive instrument, they were intended to be a point of reference for the analysis, planning, and revision of lessons and associated assessments. As certain competencies such as methodological competencies are relevant for solving problems in different subject areas, the NES also encourage the interdisciplinary cooperation of the teachers.

Of course, for the establishment of such a teaching culture to be successful, competencies in the NES need to be operationalized into actual tasks and associated items, which can be assembled into standards-based tests as well as standards-based modules for learning in schools. The different competency areas, individual competencies, and levels of competence are specified in so-called *competence models* in the NES, which can provide teachers with a frame of reference for structuring their professional action and thinking about standards-based instruction and assessment. Since competence models are academic constructs it is important that teachers be provided with concrete examples of standards-based tasks. Furthermore, empirical data from formative and summative standards-based classroom assessments and summative standards-based large-scale assessments need to be aligned with, and synthesized into, coherent descriptions of student performance in order for the NES to have a real impact on curriculum development and classroom practice. Specifically, the NES are an instrument that encourages schools and provinces to develop so-called *core curricula* that stipulate how the achievement level set by the NES could be best achieved through instructional and assessment means that focus on key content aspects and competencies in each domain and across domains.

A successful implementation of the NES thus enhances the diagnostic competence of both the teachers and the students as the NES give them specific criteria with which to measure increases in achievement and with which to develop differentiated competency profiles that can help to pinpoint areas of strength and weakness as well as potential pathways for tailored remediation. The NES also make it possible to evaluate the quality of lessons, both internally and externally.

Standards-based Quality Assurance through the Institute for Educational Progress

Parallel to the work on the standards, the *KMK Commission of Departmental Directors (KMK-Amtschefkommission)* entitled 'Quality Assurance in Schools' made preparations for the inception of the IQB. The IQB was conceived as a primarily academic institute and, as such, it needed to be part of a German university. On 4th December 2003, the KMK decided that the IQB should be institutionally bound to the Humboldt-University in Berlin. The institute is financed by the 16 federal states according to the 'Königsteiner Schlüssel'. In a

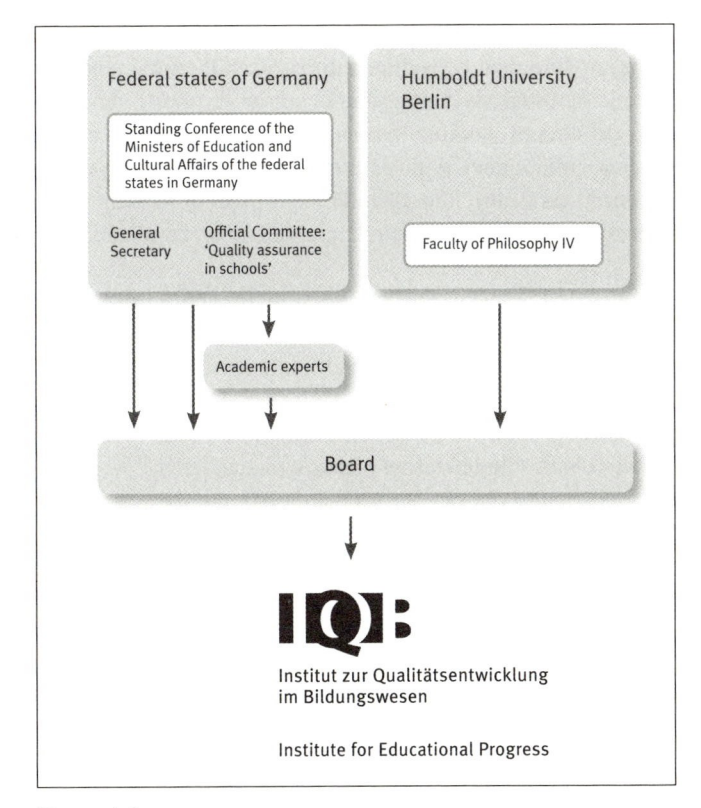

Figure 1.1
Administrative structure of the IQB.

formal resolution from 27.07.2004 the Academic Senate of the Humboldt-University Berlin approved the IQB's status as a so-called 'An-Institut' and the appointment of the institute's director, Prof. Dr. Olaf Köller, followed on 02.12.2004. The administrative structure of the IQB is shown in figure 1.

There are six different projects at the IQB that focus on the NES for different subject matters and grades. There are five projects associated with the NES for the *Hauptschulabschluss* and the *Mittlerer Schulabschluss* at the upper secondary level, (1) German, (2) mathematics, (3) natural sciences (i.e., biology, chemistry, physics), (4) English as a first foreign language, and (5) French as a first foreign language, as well as one project associated with the NES for German and mathematics at the *Primarbereich* (i.e., primary level). The core objective of each project team consists of developing large pools of standards-based test items that can be used to establish the national proficiency scales and competency levels on those scales in alignment with the NES as well as standards-based tasks for classroom instruction. The actual item writing is done by experienced teachers from the 16 federal states that are comprehensively trained by international experts in test development, a process that is described in more detail in section VI of this report.

Members of the IQB work in interdisciplinary teams coordinated by teachers with experience in the development of curricular materials and standardized achievement tests, research scientists with advanced degrees in psychology and psychometrics that act as methodological consultants to projects, doctoral students that work on project-related dissertations under the supervision of the research scientists, as well as part-time student workers that help with many aspects of the field work. Each project team collaborates with national and international experts who are involved in different areas of the item development process including the training of the item writers, the revision of the items, and the conceptualization of research studies.

In brief, the IQB pursues the aim of operationalizing the NES, providing standardized standards-based proficiency scales for each domain, assessing achievement levels on these proficiency scales, providing suggestions for further refinement of the standard documents, and supporting their implementation. This is a complex process consisting of the following component parts:
- generation of large item pools for the operationalization of standards
- development of national proficiency scales for standards-based tests
- development of computer-aided testing and reporting systems
- empirically grounded revision of theoretical competence models

In order to achieve these complex goals, research is conducted concurrently in the following areas by IQB staff in collaboration with national and international research institutions (for an overview of the latest research, please consult the associated web sites on the IQB home page at http://www.iqb.hu-berlin.de):
- Test development (*Testentwicklung*)
- Competence acquisition and development (*Kompetenzerwerb und Kompetenzentwicklung*)

- Evaluation and implementation (*Evaluation und Implementation im Schulsystem*)
- Systems monitoring for accountability purposes (*Bildungsmonitoring*)
- Research data center (*Forschungsdatenzentrum*)

Of particular importance for the portfolio of the IQB is the development of the two concurrent large item pools that are developed by the project teams described above. The first item pool consists of *standards based test items*, which are used to assemble standards-based achievement tests, which, in turn, are used to establish the national proficiency scales in alignment with the NES. In comparison to classroom tasks, test items are often less complex, especially in terms of their structure and answer format. The test item pool includes a considerable number of *selected response* items such as multiple-choice, multiple matching, or true / false / not given items in which the answer must be selected from an array of given options. In addition, many test items call for *short responses* in the form of a single word or a phrase. These items make it possible to assess students' competencies in a reliable, precise and efficient way (for a detailed discussion, see, for instance, Rupp & Vock, in press).

On the one hand, the test items developed by the IQB are used to define national proficiency scales, competence levels, and associated norms and will be used in the national extension studies starting in 2009 as discussed earlier in this section. On the other hand, they are made available to the federal states for their own independent use in standardized tests for state-wide or multi-state systems-monitoring. A small part of the items will be publicly released to illustrate their design and purpose.

The second item pool consists of *standards-based classroom tasks*, which are to be used by teachers in the classroom. They are essential for the attainment of the content and performance standards in the NES, because many of the complex competencies such as the intercultural and methodological competencies that are required for the first foreign languages need to be developed on a longer-term basis, and their attainment can only be gauged and fostered by extensive formative evaluations in the classroom itself. Through the provision of standards-based classroom tasks that are embedded in longer educational units lasting from one to several lessons, the aim is to develop a new teaching and assessment culture that extends already existing successful approaches aimed at the development and assessment of competencies. Importantly, the classroom tasks are not meant to be test items for final exams or school-leaving certificates, but, instead, they are supposed to complement existing course materials, to allow for the development of more complex competences, to foster transfer, and to evaluate learning progress in a formative fashion.

In sum, the IQB is primarily charged with the development of national proficiency scales, competency levels, and norms for all domains for which NES have been defined. The use of the scales is coupled with high expectations from educational policy makers for a reliable assessment of the profiles of student competencies within Germany. This entails the need for very high standards of test development for ensuring the construct and consequential validity of these scales and the resulting reporting mechanisms. The following sections describe the theoretical foundations, their practical realizations, and additional empirical investigations surrounding the development of the standards-based test items to illustrate how such high standards were maintained in the process.

Section II:
Foundations for Test Development

Three documents were decisive for the development of standards-based tests at the IQB. The two documents comprising the *National Educational Standards (NES)* for English as a first foreign language for the *Hauptschulabschluss* (KMK, 2004) and the *Mittlerer Schulabschluss* (KMK, 2003) as well as the *Common European Framework of Reference for Languages (CEF)* (Council of Europe, 2001). The formulations used for the NES as well as their theoretical competence model are based specifically on the CEF and its philosophy of language use, acquisition, teaching, and assessment. However, the NES and the CEF differ in terms of the scope, typology, and comprehensiveness of the described competency areas and individual competencies. These discrepancies are governed by differing political motivations. The nature of the similarities and differences between the NES and the CEF as well as their ramifications for the development of standards-based test items at the IQB are described in the following section. Since the CEF forms the basis for the NES, it will be discussed first.

The Common European Framework of Reference for Languages

The most important basis for the development of competency models and the description of competencies in the NES was the CEF. The CEF was published in 2001 and is a comprehensive synthesis of key concepts from theoretical and applied work on the foundations of language acquisition, teaching, use, and assessment. Nevertheless, arguments detailing the limitations of the CEF for the development of language tests have recently appeared in the professional literature and the interested reader is referred to authors such as Alderson et al. (2006), Little (2006), and Weir (2005) for the exact details of the perceived limitations of the CEF in different professional communities.

Political Objectives of the CEF

The aim of the CEF is to provide decision-makers involved in the acquisition, teaching, use, and assessment of language competencies with a sound academic basis for reflection of their practices. The authors wanted the CEF to be a *frame of reference* that is *user-friendly* and *descriptive* (pp. 7-8) as well as *comprehensive, transparent,* and *coherent* so that it could be used *flexibly* in order to meet the diverse demands of different stakeholders. However, the CEF does not represent a finished product for all potential purposes that could be imagined; quite to the contrary, it remains open to revision. Thus, the CEF contains no universally valid strategies or instructions for any specific use such as planning a curriculum or developing tests.

That is, the CEF is primarily an instrument for *raising awareness* of the complexities of language acquisition, teaching, use, and assessment and seeks to help experts involved in a project make overt the manifold decisions and compromises that they are making in light of these complexities to achieve the aim of their project within the real-life constraints it is set. To stimulate debates among decision-makers who use the CEF as a starting point for structuring their work, there are boxes in the CEF from chapter 4 onwards listing questions and topics that the authors of the CEF believe to be worthwhile considering in such debates. The authors of the CEF hope that an intense involvement with questions relevant to various aspects of language acquisition, teaching, use, and assessment on the basis of the CEF will eventually increase the transparency and the comparability of language courses, syllabuses, and qualifications within Europe. If such a state could be attained, then the guidelines of the Council of Europe (pp. 2-4) would be fulfilled.

The Language Model of the CEF

A core aspect of the model of language use in the CEF is reflected in its distinction of the terms *plurilingualism* and *multilingualism* (pp. 4-5). Whereas multilingualism may already be achieved, for example, by diversifying the languages that are being taught within a certain school or education system, plurilingualism can only be attained if the language competencies of one language can be integrated with competencies needed for the acquisition of another language through transfer, which creates linguistic flexibility for the language learner. In other words, multilingualism refers to the relatively objectively measurable parallelism of languages from a systems perspective whereas plurilingualism refers to the merely indirectly measurable interconnectedness of language competencies from a language user perspective.

From the aim of developing plurilingualism in Europe follows the closely connected aim of developing *pluriculturalism.* This term refers to the competence of being able to make use of integrated knowledge as well as coarse-grained language abilities and fine-grained component competencies in order to master the linguistic and non-linguistic challenges of situations in which the demands of different cultural systems and norms come together. In the CEF it is emphasized that complex pluricultural and plurilingual biographies of learners tend to evolve haphazardly and are influenced by a whole host of personal and contextual aspects throughout their lives. However, whenever learners develop plurilingual and pluricultural competencies this is expected to lead to a strongly developed sense of identity (see chapter 6.1.3, pp. 133-135). The *European Language Portfolio* (www.coe.int/portfolio) is the logical result of this philosophy. It was conceived on the basis of the CEF as a 'linguistic passport' that allows language learners in Europe to provide evidence to stakeholders that they have developed a certain level of plurilingualism and pluriculturalism.

Due to the philosophical orientation described above, the CEF is *action-orientated* and, as such, focuses predominantly on the practical ability to communicate and not on abstract knowledge of language per se. By synthesizing key theories of language structure and use (e.g., Bachman & Palmer, 1996, chapter 4), the CEF offers a model of *communicative competence* and supplies it with manifold examples. The core message of the model is as follows (see definition on p. 9 as well as chapters 4 and 5).

Effective verbal communication requires, on the one hand, competencies in four *general competency areas* (see sections 2.1.1 and 5.1):
1. declarative knowledge ('savoir'),
2. skills and know-how ('savoir-faire'),
3. existential competencies ('savoir-être'), and
4. the ability to learn or ('savoir-apprendre').

On the other hand, it requires competencies in three *communicative language competency areas* (see sections 2.1.2 and 5.2):
1. linguistic competencies,
2. sociolinguistic competencies, and
3. pragmatic competencies.

A person activates competencies in these areas, to varying degrees and in varying combinations, whenever he or she solves *complex linguistic tasks* (e.g., holding a conversation with a native speaker, formulating an e-mail; see sections 2.1.5 and 4.3) which call for certain *linguistic activities* (i.e. reception, production, interaction and mediation; see sections 2.1.3 and 4.4), which, in turn, activate *cognitive and meta-cognitive processes* (e.g., planning, execution and monitoring; see section 4.5). The linguistic activities are related to *texts* (e.g., non-fiction, video segments, charts; see sections 2.1.5 and 4.6) from specific *topics* (e.g., leisure time, shopping, applying for jobs; see section 4.2) that are located in a certain *domain* (i.e. public, private, in a working environment, and in education; see sections 2.1.4 and 4.1.1), which need to be either comprehended or produced. This takes place within the constraints of various *conditions and limitations* (i.e. physical, social and temporal; see section 4.1.3), which require the choice of appropriate and effective *strategies* (i.e. cognitive and meta-cognitive; see sections 2.1.5, 4.4.1.3, 4.4.2.4, 4.4.3.5 and 4.4.4) for a successful completion of the linguistic task by the language learner.

Scales and Competence Levels in the CEF

In order to assess the competence profile of a language learner, the CEF provides *self-assessment scales* containing empirically calibrated descriptors for the individual competence levels of the CEF, which are comprised of *can-do-statements* (for the methodology see, for example, North, 1996, 2000; North & Schneider, 1998). The CEF divides the continuum of linguistic proficiency into three basic levels (A, B and C), each of which consists of at least two primary subdivisions (1 and 2):

Table 2.1
Competence Levels of the CEF

Basic User	A	A1	Breakthrough
		A2	Waystage
Independent User	B	B1	Threshold
		B2	Vantage
Proficient User	C	C1	Effective Operational Proficiency
		C2	Mastery

The competence levels of the CEF are both generally *cumulative* and *successive*; that is to say that most of the acquired component competencies on a particular level for a particular skill are assumed to be present at the next higher level where additional competencies are added. As authors such as Alderson et al. (2006, pp. 9-13) show, however, this theoretical conception is not represented in the descriptors in a stringent fashion, which reveal inconsistencies, terminology problems, lack of definitions, and conceptual gaps.

The competence levels A1-C2 are used in different scales in the CEF. One can find, among others, (a) an overarching *global scale* (table A1, cf. CEF p. 24) that incorporates descriptors for language competence across different skills, (b) an *activity-related global scale* for self-assessment that includes descriptors for reading and listening comprehension, spoken interaction and production, as well as writing (tables A2-A4, cf. CEF pp. 26-27), (c) diverse *subscales for specific linguistic activities* in those areas (e.g., writing a letter, listening to messages; see chapter 4) and (d) diverse *subscales for specific communicative competencies* (e.g., vocabulary, grammar, phonological awareness; see chapter 5); tables C1 and C2 in the appendix show for which competencies empirically calibrated scales are available in the CEF.

The authors of the CEF emphasize, however, that the currently existing scales are merely examples and they explicitly state that they can and should be developed further, although this should be done of the basis on empirically sound descriptors (e.g., North, 2002). Furthermore, the proficiency scales can and should become more differentiated if a particular use (e.g., the development of a particular curricula or language test) makes this necessary (see chapter 3.5, pp. 31-33). This could be the case if, for example, a curriculum and associated tests are tied to a single competence level or to a small number of competence levels but inferences based on assessments require more precise differentiations between language learners.

Consequences for the Use of the CEF in Schools

In terms of the use of the CEF in schools, the CEF cannot provide a concrete manual for instruction. On the contrary, an efficient systematic linking of different actors and their actions is required in order for the CEF to fulfill its potential within an educational system. This can only happen if teachers become critically involved in discussing the core questions that the CEF evokes amongst each other and within their departments, ideally in cooperation with principals and politicians. For this purpose, the CEF provides an external and, most importantly, a neutral framework (see chapters 6.3 and 6.4).

Instead of pleading for homogeneity of concept and execution, the CEF propagates the exact opposite, namely a needs analysis of the concrete situation in an individual classroom, at a certain school, or within a certain geographic or administrative area. Thus, the proficiency scales in the CEF are merely a minor, but nonetheless important, instrument for depicting the achievement levels of learners. To be able to document the progress of language learners across the proficiency levels in a school context, more comprehensive measures need to be put in place that include formative and summative forms of evaluation tied in design, administration, scoring, and interpretation to the philosophy of the CEF.

National Educational Standards for a First Foreign Language (English/French)

Similar to the CEF, the NES for English as a first foreign language can be viewed as an invitation for stakeholders in the German educational system to get involved in a critical discourse about pathways toward developing proficiency in English and French as foreign languages with a plurilingual and pluricultural orientation. The NES remain close to the CEF in philosophy, because the formulations of the individual competencies of the learners in the NES are rooted in the descriptions of competency areas and competence levels in the CEF, which have been synthesized and adapted to suit the German educational context. Unlike the CEF, however, the NES set *normative benchmarks* for achievement because they are primarily steering instruments of educational policy. As such, they are supposed to ensure quality control, quality development, and quality assurance.

The commission and implementation of the NES reflects a shift in beliefs regarding the objectives of language acquisition, teaching, use, and assessment in schools. It reflects, above all, an orientation toward a greater degree of practical use of language based on complex communicative problems that make it possible to develop, and then assess, communicative, intercultural, and methodological competencies. Schools in general and teachers in particular need to contribute to this process by developing appropriate linguistic tasks and by providing the necessary opportunities that allow language learners in schools to become lifelong language learners so that they can develop into open-minded, tolerant, and responsible European citizens.

In other words (KMK, 2003, 2004, p. 8, translation by authors):

> [Language teaching] broadens the learners' horizons and helps them develop a greater sense of identity if their ability to compare their own views, values and social contexts with those of other cultures in a tolerant and critical manner is supported and their interest in and understanding for the way people in other cultures think and live according to their own values and norms are encouraged. Foreign language tuition mainly contributes to this multi-perspective view as part of the learners' personal development by facilitating orientation knowledge on exemplary subjects and contents and by building up intercultural communication competencies.

This quotation illustrates that it is the values that underlie the philosophy of language acquisition, teaching, use, and assessment in the CEF that should be transported through formal schooling in Germany in addition to the mere development of the competencies that are listed in the NES.

Competency Areas and Individual Competencies in the NES

The NES adapt the competency areas and individual competencies listed in the CEF into the following model of communicative competence:

Table 2.2
Competency Areas in the NES

Functional Communicative Competencies	
Communicative Skills	**Availability of Linguistic Resources**
Reading comprehension	Vocabulary
Listening and aural-visual comprehension	Grammar
Speaking	Pronunciation and Intonation
(a) Participation in conversations	Orthography / Spelling
(b) Connected speech	
Writing	
Linguistic mediation	
Intercultural Competencies	
Sociocultural orientation knowledge	
Sensitivity for cultural diversity	
Practical skills for intercultural encounters	
Methodological Competencies	
Text reception (reading comprehension and listening comprehension)	
Interaction	
Text production (speaking and writing)	
Learning strategies	
Presentation skills and skills for media usage	
Learning awareness and organization of learning processes	

The following exposition demonstrates how these competencies are linked to the competencies and competence levels of the CEF (see table A1 in the appendix). All competence descriptors in the NES are also listed for all competence areas in tables A2-A4 in the appendix where they have been numbered serially for further use.

Functional communicative competencies represent the core repertoire of linguistic abilities. *Communicative skills* include the four prototypical aspects of linguistic abilities (i.e. listening and aural-visual comprehension, reading comprehension, speaking and writing), but also the area of linguistic mediation. By contrast, the competency area entitled *availability of linguistic resources* includes those competences which comprise the basic linguistic repertoire that is necessary to establish successful communication (i.e. knowledge of vocabulary, grammar, pronunciation and intonation as well as orthography); however, they are not the focus of teaching or assessment. Relevant communication contexts, according to the NES include, among other things:

- Communicating in a first foreign language and making use of this ability in everyday life
- Making use of the knowledge gained in a first foreign language in other learning situations
- Making use of foreign language knowledge in one's career or in extended vocational training.

Thus, the area of functional communicative competencies in the NES is a blend of the general competency areas of declarative knowledge and skills and know-how as well as especially the linguistic and pragmatic communicative language competencies in the CEF.

Intercultural competencies are abilities that allow a language learner to act effectively and respectfully in situations that involve the interaction of symbols and values of different cultures. The development of intercultural competencies is, thus, not a merely cognitive exercise, but is significantly influenced by personal views and beliefs rooted in experience and ethical principles. Persons who have highly developed intercultural skills also have an insight into how their own position toward individuals from other cultures in communicative situations is culturally determined. They possess the ability and the willingness to take cognizance of other cultural perspectives and to analyze them. According to the NES, intercultural competencies mean, among others, that language learners

- know elementary specific rules of communication and interaction of selected English-speaking countries and can use the appropriate language register in familiar contexts,
- are curious about aspects foreign to them, are open to other cultures and willing to accept cultural diversity,
- are willing to adapt to new situations and to act appropriately in everyday situations,

- are able to cope with unfamiliar experiences and can handle them sensibly and appropriately,
- are not frightened of foreignness,
- are able to understand the morale and mindset in a foreign culture,
- know common views and perceptions, prejudices and stereotypes of their own country and the foreign culture and deal with them,
- can consciously perceive culture differences, misunderstandings and conflict situations, communicate about them and, if necessary, act jointly.

Intercultural competencies in the NES are based on the areas of socio-linguistic and pragmatic competences within the communicative competencies, but also on aspects of declarative knowledge as well as general abilities and procedural knowledge in the CEF.

Methodological competencies are, on the one hand, specialized and activity-specific. They are necessary for text reception (reading and listening comprehension), text production (speaking and writing), interaction, presentation, and for making use of media. On the other hand, they encompass competencies that are relevant across multiple domains such as general strategies for the organization of learning. According to the NES, this includes:
- Learning techniques and strategies for expanding on the knowledge of a foreign language as well as for the acquisition of further languages
- Developing cooperative forms of working and learning
- Achieving independence in language learning through analysis of one's personal style of learning and choice of particularly useful learning strategies
- Making use of various means of assessing spoken and written texts
- Making use of ways of user- and product-oriented structuring of spoken and written texts

Methodological competencies in the NES are based on descriptions of strategies for the linguistic activities of reception, production, interaction, and mediation and also include aspects from the general competency areas of existential knowledge and learning ability in the CEF.

Consequences for the Development of Standards-based Tests

As this brief review has demonstrated, the competence areas and individual competencies in the NES are grounded in the CEF as they were selected and adapted from the descriptions therein and rearranged into a competency model that suits the German context for standards-based language learning and standards-based assessment. As a result of the complexity of many of the competency areas, competence scales that could provide precise information for the development of test items are found neither in the CEF nor in the NES.

Thus, the challenge for the development of standards-based tests at the IQB was to operationalize the coarse-grained descriptions in the NES and in the CEF into test specifications that could guide trained item writers to produce test items that are (a) construct valid, in the sense that they are consistent with theoretical models of language competence, and (b) standard valid, in the sense that they are consistent with the formulations in the NES and the CEF. Section IV of this report is dedicated to describing how these challenges were met. Before this is done, however, section III describes another important contextual facet for the development of the standards-based test items, namely the role of English internationally and in Germany as well as the specific differences between learning English as a first, second, or foreign language.

Section III:
English Language Learning in Germany

In this section of the report, key differences between learning English as a first versus second or foreign language are surveyed, because they influence the interpretation of the resulting test scores vis-à-vis the specified constructs. Specifically, two influential factors that impact the interpretation of the results from the standards-based tests for English as a first foreign language developed at the IQB are described in the following, (a) the role of English internationally and in Germany and (b) differences in first, second, and foreign language acquisition.

As a reminder, one speaks of English as a *second language* if the language is learned by a non-native speaker of English in a country where English is spoken as the first language by most native speakers (e.g., Great Britain, the United States, Australia) while one speaks of English as a *foreign language* if the language is learned in a culture where English is not a dominant language of communication (e.g., Germany, France, Brazil, Vietnam). Alternatively, the *European Council* differentiates between (1) state languages, (2) official languages, (3) regional / minority languages, (4) non-indigenous languages, and (5) official EU languages (see Eurobarometer, 2006).

The Role of English Internationally

English is spoken as a *lingua franca* by over 1.4 billion people all over the world and is one of the native languages of some 350 million people. The regions that have the largest number of native speakers are the United States (215 million), the United Kingdom (58 million), Australia (15 million), Ireland (3.8 million), South Africa (3.7 million), New Zealand (3.5 million), and, except for the province of Québec that is predominantly Francophone, Canada (17 million). In the *European Union (EU)*, English is the most widely spoken language in 19 out of the 29 member states; 56% of Germans specifically believe that they speak English well enough to have a conversation (Eurobarometer, 2006). Of the regions where English is spoken as a second language, India is the one with the most speakers consequently giving rise to a variety known as *Indian English.* In general, there are innumerable varieties of English spoken and written across the world such that more than 42 countries where English is the primary language and more than 28 countries where English is one of the official languages are currently listed on reference sites like Wikipedia (www.wikipedia.org).

A few standardized versions of English exist, which include *Standard American English*, *Standard British English*, *Standard Canadian English*, and *Standard Australian English*. These have been moulded by the practical uses of the native and non-native speakers in these countries over several centuries and codified in publications such as the *Oxford English Dictionary*, *Webster's Collegiate Dictionary*, and *Quirk's University Grammar*, as well as pronunciation dictionaries with the one by Daniel Jones for British English being the classic example. Standardized versions are typically most appealing for teaching purposes, because they represent a relatively stable system and are accepted by prestigious media organizations and business professionals as the preferred linguistic standard of communication.

However, the selection of one of these standards typically entails a teaching focus on a particular country such as Great Britain or the U.S. with its diverse cultural system. Without doubt, English has become the language of international business, of information technology, and international research fuelled by an ever-increasing trend of economic and cultural globalization and human interconnectedness. Consequently, it accounts for large portions of professional communication via e-mails, letters, faxes, telephones, cell phones, BlackBerries, audio conferences, and video conferences.

The Role of English in Germany

Students in Germany learn *English as a foreign language* only, which implies that their exposure to authentic English texts, either orally or in print, is restricted (see, e.g., Finkenstaedt & Schröder, 1991; Eurobarometer, 2006). However, there is a tendency of introducing English chunks and phrases into advertisements that are printed or shown in German, and English is being used increasingly for signs and announcements in metropolises such as Berlin, Frankfurt, and Munich. Yet, English is not spoken on a day-to-day basis in German society. Simplified varieties of English are sometimes used in Germany as a lingua franca within neighbourhoods that have a high ethnic diversity but students typically have either very limited or even no opportunities to practice spoken or written production and interaction in English outside the school context.

Schooling, thus, represents one important opportunity for students to be exposed to authentic texts even though the degree to which texts could be considered as authentic differs depending on the type of textbook used and the materials selected by the individual teacher (for a critical discussion of authenticity we refer the reader to Gilmore, 2007). Similarly, the degree to which problem-solving contexts in school reflect genuine contexts outside of school is debatable and varies highly across classrooms. Nevertheless, almost half of all Germans believe that the best place to learn a foreign language is school (Eurobarometer, 2006, QA7b). As a result, learning environments in schools should be as authentic as possible, not only linguistically but also culturally, to support the development of functional language competencies as required by the CEF and the NES.

In Germany, English is predominantly learned as the first foreign language starting in 5th grade. A recent policy decision to make French the mandatory first language in the state of Baden-Württemberg – due to its geographic proximity to France – caused significant public disapproval (Der Spiegel, 2007) and the decision was eventually reversed. This reflects the common parental belief that English is the most critical language that helps their children to build the foundation for a successful and rich professional and personal development later in life. Similarly, 82% of Germans believe that knowing at least one foreign language could be very useful personally (Eurobarometer, 2006, p. 28), 89% believe that one of these languages should be English (Eurobarometer, 2006, Q2Ab), and 62% of Germans are further willing to agree that all official communication in the EU should take place in one common language (Eurobarometer, 2006, p. 55), which would most likely be English also.

To further understand the role of English in German schools for the development of the standards-based tests at the IQB, it is essential to understand that large parts of Germany have a predominantly tripartite system at the secondary level. It consists of the grammar school (*Gymnasium*) as the track leading to the highest school-leaving qualification, the *Abitur*, after 12 or 13 years of schooling, the higher middle school (*Realschule*) leading to the middle-tier school-leaving qualification, the *Mittlerer Schulabschluss*, after 10 years of schooling, and the lower middle school (*Hauptschule*) leading to the lower-tier school-leaving qualification, the *Hauptschulabschluss*, after 9 years of schooling. Despite an early tracking of students after primary school (i.e., after 4th or 6th grade depending on the state), there are indications that the German school system is slowly opening. Put differently, it is slowly becoming possible to obtain the school-leaving qualification *Mittlerer Schulabschluss*, to which one set of NES is tied, in a wider variety of school forms other than the prototypical *Realschule* (see Cortina et al., 2003).

Due to the different orientations of the three prototypical school tracks, different student populations and objectives for learning English exist in the tracks. Whereas grammar school is a type of school where aspects of general education (*Allgemeinbildung*) are transported through foreign language tuition, the *Hauptschule*, in contrast, is much more oriented toward the blue-collar labour market; as a result, foreign language teaching, though introduced in the 1950s, plays less of a central role in this track. At the same time, the *Hauptschule* typically represents the widest mix of non-native speakers of German due to its blend of students from various cultures and migrant backgrounds. Consequently, teachers in English courses in a *Hauptschule* are faced with numerous challenges that are non-linguistic such as motivation, attention, and behavioural problems as well as a lack of resources outside of school that could compensate for the schooling difficulties. Therefore, the average level of English proficiency is generally lowest in the *Hauptschule*, higher in the *Realschule*, and highest in the Gymnasium, especially among those students who choose English as one of their A-level courses where they have five hours of English per week (see Beck & Klieme, 2007).

Despite the restricted access to authentic materials in schools and real-life opportunities to interact with native speakers of English as well as the challenges inherent in the tripartite school system at the secondary level, there are important resources that students can draw on to practice their English skills. In larger German cities such as Munich, Frankfurt, Hamburg, or Berlin, for example, international magazines and newspapers in English are relatively easily available at international newsstands. Furthermore, some German publications such as *Der*

Spiegel now produce English-language special editions once in a while and have created international websites in English (http://www.spiegel.de/international).

Probably the dominant sources for English texts of all sorts for learners are popular media anyway. Most importantly, these include internet web sites but also films in original language in movie theatres or on DVD, music on CDs or internet platforms, podcasts of international music, TV, or radio programs that can be downloaded online, as well as internet chat rooms and online blogs. An interesting recent development that might significantly impact the learning of interaction skills of students is the creation of *Second Life* (http://secondlife.com), the virtual world where people from all over the world can create alter egos, so-called avatars, and interact freely with others in a fictitious 3-D environment. Users have started to recreate real places in this virtual world and many companies have gone so far as to create virtual dependencies that include well-respected institutions such as the most renowned scientific journal *Nature*. Hence, the lack of interactional opportunities of students in a real-world city might be partially compensated for by interactional opportunities in virtual city segments of these cities in *Second Life*.

In a nutshell, learning English as a foreign language and the signifiers of the cultures where it plays an important role for private, educational, or commercial communication will more and more be based on a kaleidoscopic hybrid of multi-media materials and interactions with others via the internet, especially in writing. Importantly, using these resources for personal pleasure might occupy a large part of leisure time outside school for some students, which represents an important aspect of language learning even though it would most likely not be classified as such by the students themselves. The degree to which students can make use of this exposure to actively improve their language skills beyond a certain learning plateau requires further research, however.

Caveats of this process need to be noted. From the perspective of the development of reading and listening comprehension competences, of media skills, and of intercultural sensitivity, internet sites and forums may be the largest reservoir of English-language material and they are easy to access for most students. Consequently, the internet is now also being widely used as an additional source of teacher information and a tool for student research. Nevertheless, the range of cultural references clearly represents only a section of the broad linguistic and cultural experiences in the countries where English is a dominant language and is often a snapshot of current pop culture. Especially on internet sites used for entertainment or other leisure activities, the linguistic complexity, accuracy, and pragmatic appropriateness of the texts can vary widely so that only more proficient students are likely to benefit from this added exposure to English due to advanced monitoring and self-regulation skills.

Finally, it should also be noted that a growing number of students take advantage of improving their intercultural and linguistic skills in real-life environments through language travel. Specifically, more than 89% of German students reported in 2005 that they travel to learn English rather than a different language and 54.7% of students travelled to Great Britain while only 2.25% travel to the

U.S.; however, the mean travel time is only between two and three weeks (FDSV, 2006). A smaller number of students are spending a year abroad during school (e.g., studying a year at a U.S. High School) or take an extended trip into an English-speaking country for personal growth after high-school graduation, which may help to account for exceptional performance of some of these students in certain domains.

Differences in First, Second, and Foreign Language Acquisition

There is an abundance of literature on different aspects and subtleties of second or foreign versus first language acquisition captured in several academic journals (e.g., Second Language Acquisition, Second Language Learning), numerous foundational books (e.g., Doughty & Long, 2005; Ellis & Widdowson, 1997; Gass & Selinker, 2001; Schachter, 1990), and a wide variety of didactic books (e.g., Brown, 1994; Byram, 1997). The major differences between second and foreign language learning is the exposure to authentic materials and linguistic problem-solving situations with native speakers, which was discussed in the previous subsection. In contrast, some of the main differences between first and second language learners that account for qualitative processing differences and quantitative performance differences were succinctly summarized by Enright et al. (2000) in the context of the development of a reading comprehension assessment and are reviewed here briefly.

Second language learners are strongly influenced by their overall ability and the processing experiences made in the first language and will try to utilize existing first language structures and strategies as much as possible for second language tasks. Hence, they will often process second-language tasks cross-linguistically by drawing on knowledge and skills acquired in their first language as well as other second or foreign languages. Thus, the perception of task difficulty in a second language depends crucially on the similarities and differences between the first and second language. Consequently, second language learners are prone to positive and negative transfer effects as they have a different vocabulary size and structure than native speakers based on a more limited knowledge of cultural situations and authentic language use situations. These limited exposures hinder the establishment of visual-graphic relationships in memory leading many second language learners to focus more on irrelevant information in texts, especially at early stages of second language learning. As a result, they encounter more frustration-level texts, but also have many supporting materials such as glossaries, dictionaries, and grammar books at their disposal. Since they are motivated for different reasons than native speakers to learn the language, they typically possess higher degrees of meta-cognitive awareness generally and meta-linguistic awareness specifically due to a more formal approach to language learning.

PISA, PIRLS, and DESI have shown that the language that is spoken at home is typically the first language of one or both of the parents. As a result, there are three major subpopulations in Germany that need special consideration with regards to foreign language learning. The first subpopulation consists of German-born children where both parents are German; these children almost certainly speak German at home. The second subpopulation consists of German- or foreign-born children from families where one of the two parents is non-German; these children may speak the language of either parent at home. The third subpopulation consists of German- or foreign-born children from families where both parents are non-German; these children almost certainly speak the first language of the parent(s) at home. For some children in subpopulation two and all children in subpopulation three German is their second language and English is either the second foreign language or one of several foreign languages. Hence, only the effects of the structural similarities between German and English are relevant for understanding performance differences of children from the first subpopulation while the pair-wise structural similarities between the first language, German, and English need to be taken into account for understanding performance differences for some children in the second subpopulation and all children in the third subpopulation.

Moreover, depending on the neighbourhoods in which children grow up, the language spoken with friends can vary significantly too. The migrant population in Germany is relatively diverse with Turkish immigrants or second-generation families accounting for the largest portion (almost 40%) followed by migrants from former Yugoslavia (14%), Italy (13%), and Greece (6%). Semilingual levels of proficiency and pidginized forms of language have lately evolved, and there are now definite signs of a 'Türkendeutsch', which may very well develop into a sub-standard German creole in the next few decades. Thus, in order to fully understand error patterns and proficiency differences between students, the type of native language that is spoken by them, their parents, and their friends in their larger social milieu is indispensable.

Implications for the Development of Standards-based Tests

The primary consequence of the role of English internationally and in Germany as well as differences in first, second and foreign language learning for the development of the standards-based test at the IQB is that the processing models commonly assumed for reading comprehension, listening comprehension, or writing in a first language cannot be *a priori* transferred to a second or foreign language testing context. Specifically, if students are asked to make complex inferences and form elaborate mental models of either orally or visually presented texts, tight time constraints can pose a problem for measuring the true language ability of second language learners with different first languages due to differences in adapted cognitive processes. Consequently, items were pre-tested with diverse samples to establish realistic mean response times for completion of test sections.

From a content perspective, Great Britain rates highest amongst the countries where German students would spend or already have spent some time for leisure or educational purposes. Given the specific European focus of the CEF as adopted by the NES, it was decided to predominantly focus on the cultural contexts and standardized English varieties of Great Britain as the main – albeit not exclusive – reference point for developing the standards-based tests at the IQB. Hence, many of the images and illustrations, names, places, and references were taken from diverse sources on the internet and contain cultural symbols that are typical of Britain and reflect situations that need to be commonly encountered by native and non-native speakers in this country. Furthermore, statistical analyses of the resulting scales will be conducted with particular attention paid to learners from various linguistic backgrounds to eliminate biases for these groups due to the construction of the test questions, the selection of the texts, or the requested type of text. In the documentation of the tests, guides will be included for teachers that exemplify how diagnostic information can be culled from standards-based test questions about the possible reasons for certain errors made by learners with diverse linguistic backgrounds.

Section IV:
Test Specifications

Synopsis

The standards-based tests developed by the IQB achievement tests in English as a first foreign language based on the German National Educational Standards (NES) for the Hauptschulabschluss (KMK, 2004) and for the Mittlerer Abschluss (KMK, 2003). The tests are administered in paper-and-pencil format to classes of students who are randomly selected to participate. There are strict time constraints for each test form and each block of items within each test form; the amount of time is estimated by item developers and IQB test administrators to be sufficient to prevent strong speed effects. The item characteristics of most items in the item pool were empirically investigated on a large-scale basis for the first time during a field trial between April and May 2007 in which about 3000 students participated. The final proficiency scales for the standards-based test will be created based on the item calibrations of the main trial during April and May 2008 in which about 6000 students will participate. Various types of documentation for the proficiency scales based on comprehensive psychometric and expert analyses will be made publicly available for different stakeholders in 2009. As part of this documentation, further volumes in this technical report series will be released.

The item pool that has been developed for the standards-based tests consists of *selected- and constructed-response items* that are dichotomously scored (i.e., that receive a score of '0' or '1' for 'incorrect' or 'correct' answers) for the reading and listening comprehension sections as well as *extended constructed response tasks* for writing that are *polytomously* rated (i.e., that receive graded scores like '0', '1', '2', or '3' by multiple raters).

At the time of the publication of this report, the item writers had developed a total of 551 reading comprehension items associated with 99 tasks / testlets, 429 listening comprehension items associated with 78 tasks / testlets, and 86 writing tasks between September 2005 and July 2007 and the field trial had just been completed. In the field trial, 393 reading comprehension items associated with 71 tasks / testlets, 352 listening comprehension items associated with 65 tasks / testlets, and 19 writing prompts were utilized corresponding to 71%, 82%, and 22% of the items in the pool.

The items were distributed across different *booklets* using a *matrix-sampling* or *balanced incomplete block design*. Consequently, each student worked only on a selected number of items, but all student responses can be linked onto a common scale for reading and listening comprehension as well as writing using psychometric methods from *item response theory*. In most cases, each student responded to two blocks with reading comprehension items for a total of 40 minutes, two blocks with listening comprehension items for a total of 40 minutes, and two blocks with writing tasks for a total of 40 minutes; some students respond to one longer block of 60 minutes with writing tasks coupled with one shorter block of 20 minutes for one of the other two skills. All students also responded to a test of general cognitive ability for a total of 20 minutes as well as self-report questionnaires, which required them to provide selected-response or open-ended answers, for a total of 40 minutes. Consequently, students were assessed for a total of 180 minutes, which resulted in a total session time of about 240 minutes including short breaks. No personally identifying information about the students was kept as anonymous identification numbers were used. The structure of the main trial will be similar to the structure of the field trial.

Test Purpose

The purpose of the standards-based achievement tests developed by the IQB is to operationalize the content and performance standards for English as a first foreign language as outlined in the German *National Educational Standards (NES)* for the *Hauptschulabschluss* (KMK, 2004) and for the *Mittlerer Abschluss* (KMK, 2003).

Resulting Proficiency Scales

The product of this process is the creation of a global *proficiency scale* for English as well as separate *subscales* for *reading comprehension, listening comprehension,* and *writing*. Through the process of *standard-setting* (e.g., Cizek, Bunch, & Coons, 2004; Zieky & Perie, 2006) and associated psychometric analyses of item characteristics (e.g., Hartig & Frey, 2005; Rost, 2004), *cut-scores* will be determined for each proficiency scale, which distinguish students according to the *proficiency levels* of the *Common European Framework of Reference for Languages (CEF)* (Council of Europe, 2001). For all scales provided by the IQB, the maximum number of proficiency levels among which a reliable differentiation of students can be made is five (i.e., A1, A2, B1, B2, and C1). This omits the level C2 as the highest level of proficiency distinguished in the CEF, which indexes a proficiency level that is expected to be too advanced for a sufficiently large number of German students to allow for a reliable classification.

The publication of the proficiency scales will be accompanied with the release of two different pools of standards-based test items. The first pool of *confidential test items* will be made available only to the 16 individual states and their schools, which can use them for any type of standardized achievement testing that suits their purpose. The second pool of *non-confidential test items* will be available to anyone seeking examples of standards-based tasks through the internet website of the IQB including parents, students, and teachers. The latter pool of items does not overlap with the pool of confidential items used by the individual states and by the IQB, but is consistent in design with this pool. Specifically, the range of competencies, proficiency levels, content areas, and cognitive operations of the items in the non-confidential item pool is similar to that of the items in the confidential item pool.

Resulting Decisions about Students

The *field trial* in 2007 and the *main trial* in 2008 are designed for two aligned purposes. First, both trials are necessary to establish the proficiency scales psychometrically. The sample of students that is used to establish the final proficiency scales in the main trial is a large, random, and representative sample of students from all 16 federal states in Germany and represents the full range of student diversity on such key variables as ethnicity, sex, socioeconomic statuses, and school type.

Both trials place primary importance on *item characteristics and the establishment of unidimensional proficiency scales for each skill* rather than the reporting of differentiated competency profiles of students. The main trial in 2008, in particular, is used to ascertain the psychometric properties of the resulting proficiency scales based on items that were revised after the field trial in 2007 and augmented with previously untested items from the item pool. The proficiency scales that result from this process will be used in future extension studies for accountability purposes to report on the distribution of student competencies across the 16 federal states.

Specifically, as outlined in Section I of this report, nationally representative random samples will be used to compare the performance of students and schools across the 16 federal states starting in the year 2009, which will replace the PISA extension studies that were conducted in 2000, 2003, and 2006 (see KMK, 2006). At the time of writing, no definitive political decisions have been made as to what the consequences for students, schools, states or other stakeholders of this comparison will be. The reporting of student proficiencies on the four scales (i.e., English language ability, reading comprehension, listening comprehension, and writing) in the future is likely to be primarily descriptive and, thus, *low-stakes* from the perspective of the students as well as their parents, teachers, and schools. While it is currently not envisioned that decisions about individual students will be made in the future on the basis of the proficiency scales due to the psychometric unreliability of such decisions, descriptive comparisons of students groups at different levels of aggregation (e.g., classes, schools, states) will be made on the basis of predictor variables known to be related to school performance such as school type, sex, ethnic background, and socio-economic status.

Other Tests Linked to the CEF

Internationally, there are a variety of tests for English as a foreign language that are linked to the CEF, which can be compared to the standards-based tests developed at the IQB. Notably, the linkage of these tests has been established differently for different tests. For some tests, it has been established only after they had been in use for a while. For others, it has been established from first principles, because the tests were explicitly developed with reference to the CEF descriptions of language proficiency and their associated descriptors; this was also the case with the standards-based tests developed by the IQB. In this section of the report, the tests that are most frequently used in practice or referred to in research on CEF linkage will be reviewed and compared and contrasted with the standards-based tests developed by the IQB.

The Cambridge ESOL Exams

The largest test battery for English as a foreign language at different age levels was developed at the University of Cambridge by the working group called *English for Speakers of Other Languages (ESOL)*. The tests developed by the Cambridge ESOL group are taken by more than two million people in over 130 countries each year. Since the group is a member of the *Association of Language Testers in Europe (ALTE)* (www.alte.org) its tests adhere to their internationally recognized *Code of Practice* (http://www.alte.org/quality_assurance/index.php). Various tests are available for English language learners seeking an assessment of their general language ability, specific components of their language ability, or specific language varieties such as business English, professional English, or academic English.

The tests of general English comprise the *Cambridge Young Learners English Tests (YLE)*, which are targeted at levels A2, A1, and below; the *Key English Test (KET)*, which is targeted at level A2, the *Preliminary English Test (PET)*, which is targeted at level B1; the *First Certificate in English (FCE)*, which is targeted at level B2; the *Certificate in Advanced English (CAE)*, which is targeted at level C1; and the *Certificate in Proficiency in English (CPE)*, which is targeted at level C2. Tests for component skills of general English language ability include first and foremost the *Certificates in English Language Skills (CELS)* targeted at levels B1 to C1 but also the *Certificates in ESOL Skills for Life*, which are of a more limited use only for learners in England, Wales, and Northern Ireland.

Tests for business English include the *Business English Certificates (BEC)* targeted at level B1 to C1 and the *Business Language Testing Service (BULATS)* while tests for professional English include the *International Legal English Certificate (ILEC)* and the *International Certificate in Financial English (ICFE)* depending on the area of specialization needed. For academic English there is the *International English Language Testing System (IELTS)*. It is a comprehensive international testing system (see www.ielts.org) for people who intend to study or work in a place where English is the dominant language of communication. The tests in the IELTS are thus seen, by some, as competitors to other established tests such as the TOEFL, which measures English language proficiency at levels B1 to C1 for university-level learners and is discussed in more detail below, or the UNIcert tests, which measure English and other language proficiencies at levels B1 to C2 for university-level learners in Germany (http://rcswww.urz.tu-dresden.de/~unicert/index.htm).

Most English language tests of the ESOL group have been linked to the CEF in a long-term project on investigating the theoretical potential and practical limitations of the *Manual* (Kaftandjieva et al., 2004); the relationship between the difficulty range of each test and the CEF proficiency levels are shown in figure 4.1 (see www.cambridgeesol.org).

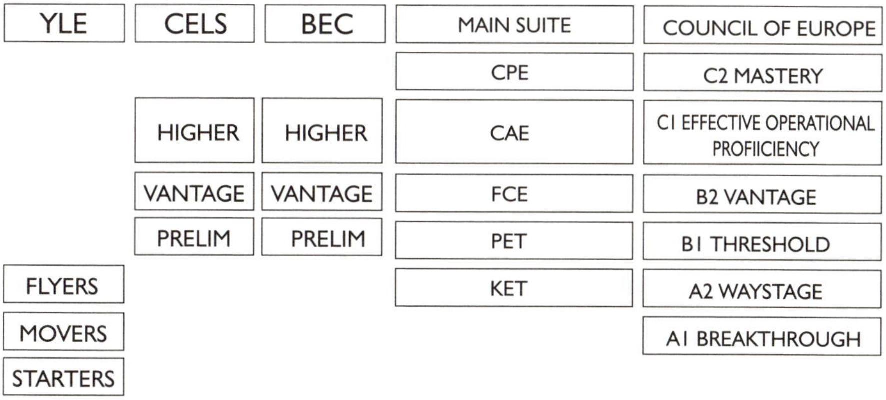

YLE	CELS	BEC	MAIN SUITE	COUNCIL OF EUROPE
			CPE	C2 MASTERY
	HIGHER	HIGHER	CAE	C1 EFFECTIVE OPERATIONAL PROFICIENCY
	VANTAGE	VANTAGE	FCE	B2 VANTAGE
	PRELIM	PRELIM	PET	B1 THRESHOLD
FLYERS			KET	A2 WAYSTAGE
MOVERS				A1 BREAKTHROUGH
STARTERS				

Figure 4.1
Relationship of individual ESOL tests with proficiency levels in the CEF.

The TOEFL

The *Test of English as a Foreign Language (TOEFL)* is one of the most commonly taken and used tests internationally as it is recognized by more than 6000 institutions in over 110 countries worldwide. It is developed by the *Educational Testing Service (ETS)* (www.ets.org) with headquarters in Princeton, NJ, in the U.S., which is the world's largest non-profit research organization whose research focuses on all aspects of test development processes.

The TOEFL test had been transferred from its original paper-and-pencil format (*TOEFL-PBT*) to a computer-based test version (*TOEFL-CBT*) whose administration was ceased in 2006, however, and has been replaced by an internet-based test version (*TOEFL-iBT*). The TOEFL-iBT is a *computerized adaptive test* that assesses the four key skills reading comprehension (60-100 minutes, 36-70 items), listening comprehension (60-90 minutes, 34-51 items), writing (50 minutes, 2 tasks), and speaking (20 minutes, 6 tasks). Historically, the writing section in the TOEFL-CBT was referred to as the *Test of Written English (TWE)* but is now integrated into the TOEFL-iBT.

The structure of the iBT is based on a redesign of the TOEFL-PBT and TOEFL-CBT that is documented in a series of research reports that describe this process overall (Jamieson et al., 2000) as well as its domain-specific realizations for reading comprehension (Enright et al., 2000), listening comprehension (Bejar et al., 2000), writing (Cumming et al., 2000), and speaking (Butler et al., 2000).

In its current form, the TOEFL-iBT test measures

> "[…] the communicative language ability of people whose first language is not English. It will measure examinees' English- language proficiency in situations and tasks reflective of university life in North America. […] Scale scores are designed to be used as one criterion in decision-making for undergraduate and graduate admissions." (Jamieson et al., 2000, p. 19).

In contrast to the standards-based tests developed at the IQB, the TOEFL-iBT test is, thus, designed for an older population of learners, which is formally described on the website as 'learners at an 11th-grade level of education', but especially comprises students in their late teens as well as twenties. Moreover, the content of the test as well as the genres and rhetorical structures that are covered with the test are narrower than those of the IQB tests, because they focus on academic life and work in the U.S. only. Consequently, the standard language is *American English*. Note-taking is allowed on all sections and texts or input has been selected to be as authentic as possible while adhering to the test specifications. Even though the language model of *communicative competence* or *communicative ability* underlying the TOEFL-iBT test is similar to that of the CEF, it does not follow the philosophical orientation of the CEF toward an interconnectedness of multiple languages geared toward developing plurilingual and pluricultural competencies. Hence, non-cognitive competencies such as intercultural competencies play a small role in the development of the TOEFL.

In 2005, the TOEFL-PBT and TWE were linked to the CEF via a standard-setting study (Tannenbaum & Wylie, 2005) along with the *Test of English for International Communication (TOEIC)* and the *Test of Spoken English (TSE)*. Quite simply, it was determined that all four tests cover levels B1 to C1 of the CEF and also allow for a statement that a learner is *below B1* if his or her score does not exceed the cut-score for B1. However, there are problems with this linkage. For example, the bands for B1-B2 and C1 on the TWE are unjustifiably small as they range from 4.5 to 5.5 points and 5.5 to 6 points, respectively, while the band for 'below B1' ranges from 1 to 4.5 points causing doubt at the defensibility of these cut scores. The cut scores for the TOEFL-PBT divide the score band up into wider score bands with the one for 'below B1' ranging from 310 to 457 points, the band for B1 and B2 ranging from 457 to 560 points, and the band for C1 ranging from 560 to 677 points, which may be more defensible than the TWE cut scores. Nevertheless, the linkage is based on one standard-setting study only and is not widely published suggesting that ETS itself seems to be doubting the reliability of this linkage.

The DIALANG System

The DIALANG system is a freely available language assessment suite for 14 common languages in the EU (i.e., Danish, Dutch, English, Finnish, French,

German, Greek, Icelandic, Irish, Italian, Norwegian, Portuguese, Spanish, and Swedish) (for detailed descriptions of the system see Alderson, 2005; Alderson & Huhta, 2005). The system is developed to be low-stakes for the learners. It is *highly flexible* in that it allows learners to take charge of their learning as they can decide freely whether to take a self-assessment and / or vocabulary placement test, which language they would like the instructions to be presented in, which subtests they want to take, and when they want to quit the system. It is *diagnostic*, because learners can choose to have immediate feedback that is presented on the screen after each item.

The system is *adaptive at the test level*, because learners are presented with a main language test that matches their general proficiency level as assessed by the placement test(s) (i.e., levels A, B, or C of the CEF); if learners skip the placement test(s), they will be given a language test at level B. All test results are presented in terms of the proficiency levels of the CEF as there are tests for all languages at all six proficiency levels. However, it needs to be remembered that the DIALANG development was complex due to the high level of international collaboration that involved countries with varying levels of experience in the development of standardized large-scale language tests, especially those linked to the CEF. Consequently, the quality of empirical evidence that could be gathered for the individual language tests varied widely and the degree to which it is trustworthy for a given language test needs much more additional empirical investigation (Alderson & Huhta, 2005; see also Chapelle, 2006).

The Trinity College GESE and ISE Exams

The *Graded Examinations in Spoken English (GESE)* and the *Integrated Skills in English (ISE)* language assessments are developed by the *Trinity College* in London. The GESE is an exam of speaking skills available for four different grade bands that cover grades 1-12 (*Initial*: 1-3, *Elementary*: 4-6, *Intermediate*: 7-9, *Advanced*: 10-12) (Trinity College London, 2005a); each test is more comprehensive than the previous one. For example, while the *Initial* assessment for grades 1-3 takes only between 5-7 minutes and assesses conversation skills only, the *Advanced* assessment for grades 10-12 takes 25 minutes and assesses skills in listening comprehension, conversation, topic presentation and discussion, and also contains an interactive task. The ISE is an integrated assessment with four levels (*ISE 0, ISE I, ISE II, ISE III*) that consists of tasks with performance expectations that are aligned with those in selected grade levels for the GESE (Trinity College London, 2005b). The ISE also contains a portfolio task and an integrative task for reading and writing. Thus, the ISE measures all four basic skills of speaking, listening, reading, and writing.

Both the GESE and ISE assessments have recently been linked to the CEF in a comprehensive project whose structure follows the *Manual* and involved 12 experts (Papageorgiou, 2007). Generally speaking, the GESE suite covers the entire range of CEF levels while the ISE assessments cover levels A2 to C1; table 4.1 shows the specific correspondences for the GESE (from pp. 29, 31, 64) and table 4.2 shows the specific correspondences for the ISE (from pp. 30, 31, 65).

Table 4.1
Linkage of the Trinity College GESE Exam to the CEF

GESE Level	Grade	CEF Level (Content Classification)	CEF Level (Standard-setting)
Initial	1	A1	*A1*
	2	A1 – A2	*A1+*
	3	A2.1	*A2*
Elementary	4	A2.2	*A2+*
	5	B1.1	*B1*
	6	B1.2	*B1+*
Intermediate	7	B2.1	*B2*
	8	B2.1 – B2.2	*B2+*
	9	B2.1 – B2.2	*B2+*
Advanced	10	B2.2 – C1	*C1*
	11	C1	*C1*
	12	C1 – C2	*C2*

Note. The standard-setting result is the result of the second round of judgments and refers to a secure 'pass' on the exam.

Table 4.2
Linkage of the Trinity College GESE Exam to the CEF

ISE Level	CEF Level (Content Classification)	CEF Level (Standard-setting)
ISE 0	A2 – B1.1	*A2+*
ISE I	B1.1 – B1.2	*B1*
ISE II	B2.1 – B2.2	*B2*
ISE III	C1	*C1*

Note. The standard-setting result is the result of the second round of judgments and refers to a 'pass' for a borderline learner on the exam.

Importantly, learners receive a compensatory binary composite score on both the GESE and the ISE so that the CEF levels in the tables are levels for the composite score. Consequently, learners may receive a composite score that is a 'pass' and places them at a certain CEF level, but this could be a result of mixed levels of language proficiency, especially lower levels of language proficiency, for some subtests.

Since the steps for linking the GESE and ISE assessments to the CEF as described in the *Manual* have been followed meticulously, have been corroborated with internal and external validation studies, at least in general, and have been documented in great detail, this linkage appears to be rather trustworthy and seems to be a good model for other post-hoc linkage projects.

The Tests of the DESI Study

The DESI study was commissioned by the KMK and conducted by an international consortium of experts in language testing and didactics. The tests in DESI assess reading comprehension, listening comprehension, writing, and speaking and are geared toward levels A1 to B2+ of the CEF. They were developed for students in grade 9 across different school types based on a detailed analysis of the German curricula for teaching English as a foreign language in grades 8 and 9 across all 16 federal states. The field test data were collected in 2002 with a sample of approximately 1200 students from all 16 federal states in Germany and the subsequent calibration studies were conducted in 2003 and 2004 with samples of 10639 and 10632 students, respectively (Beck & Klieme, 2007; Jude & Klieme, 2007; see Harsch, 2005).

The construct of reading comprehension focuses on the ability to comprehend different aspects of expository texts, which means narrative texts generally and drama texts specifically. The different types of reading comprehension that were assessed can be classified as (a) understanding specific details, (b) understanding relationships between elements in a text, and (c) reflecting on and interpreting texts. Moreover, cognitive processes in reading comprehension were empirically mapped onto the items by modelling item difficulty as a function of six task characteristics (Nold & Willenberg, 2007b, pp. 262-231).

The construct of listening comprehension focuses on the ability to comprehend classroom talk as well as scripted texts that resemble literate adapted texts. Shorter dialogues in DESI contained more elements of natural unedited speech in informal contexts, but not in the same frequency and breadth as truly authentic texts. The different types of listening comprehension that were assessed can be classified as (a) understanding specific details, (b) understanding the main idea, (c) recognizing key content elements in other contexts that use circumscriptions and synonyms, (d) reflecting on and interpreting texts. As in reading comprehension, cognitive processes in listening comprehension were empirically mapped onto the items by modelling item difficulty as a function of six task characteristics (Nold & Rossa, 2007a, pp. 208-216).

The construct of writing focuses on productive and interactive writing tasks on a variety of topics from narrative and expository genres. The written texts were rated holistically as well as according to the three different analytic criteria that are composites of nine criteria at a finer level of detail: (a) overall impression / communicative effect, (b) task-specific features, and (c) language use (Harsch, 2005, chapter 4; Harsch et al., 2007, pp. 66-68). More details on the DESI study can be found in the following section of this report.

Section V:
Construct Definitions

In this section of the technical report, the construct definitions for the standards-based tests developed by the IQB are developed for *reading comprehension*, *listening comprehension*, and *writing* are described in detail. Each subsection starts with a brief discussion of the complexities involved in assessing these constructs in large-scale assessments generally. The definition for each respective construct is then developed based on a synthesis of information from three sources:
1. the National Educational Standards (NES) (KMK, 2003, 2004) and the Common European Framework for Languages (CEF) (Council of Europe, 2001),
2. the relevant research literature, and
3. the construct definition in the German DESI German acronym for (Deutsch-Englisch Schülerleistungen International) study (e.g., Beck & Klieme, 2007).

The construct definitions for the standards-based tests developed by the IQB are then provided at the end of each subsection.

Reading Comprehension

The Assessment of Reading Comprehension in Large-scale Assessments

A variety of methods have been used to assess reading comprehension in large-scale assessments (see, e.g., Alderson, 2000; Alderson & Banerjee, 2002). In contrast to listening comprehension assessments, the stimulus for reading comprehension tasks is available for review allowing test-takers to utilize a variety of reading strategies in a test-taking situation that are reflective of natural reading (e.g., re-reading, underlining, commenting). The assessment of reading comprehension with the standards-based tests developed by the IQB is similar to that of other large-scale studies on basic literacy or reading achievement. For comparative purposes, table C4 in the appendix shows the reading comprehension skills that have been assessed in different waves of large-scale assessments conducted in Germany since the 1990s. The construct definitions in the studies listed in table C4 are grounded in comprehensive reviews of the literature on reading comprehension processes. Essentially, all construct definitions are based on a blend of a cognitive processing, reader purpose, and reading task perspective as compared and contrasted by Enright et al. (2000).

A *cognitive processing perspective* describes the mental operations necessary for successful reading comprehension on different items. Thus, it is not very useful for designing test specifications due to the high level of cognitive granularity. That is, while interpretations about responses to reading comprehension items should be commensurate with cognitive models of reading comprehension, they can rarely provide detailed information about the involved processes unless meticulous validation studies are conducted. These, however, are typically restricted in their generality by small sample sizes as a consequence of resource constraints.

A *reading task perspective* focuses on the real-life tasks that proficient readers can perform in authentic contexts. Within a testing context – where the use of complex tasks in authentic situations is typically prohibitive due to costs and logistics associated with development and administration – the reading task perspective is used to identify the critical linguistic features of these tasks and to evaluate the degree to which texts and items on the tests are similar in their composition to their real-life counterparts. Thus, agencies that develop large-scale assessments utilize this perspective when they code the characteristics of texts and items that are believed to influence the empirical characteristics of the items such as their difficulty or discrimination.

Research has identified a variety of variables that are able to account for item characteristics on reading comprehension tests (e.g., Buck, Tatsuoka, & Kostin, 1997; Freedle & Kostin, 1991, 1992, 1993; Gorin, 2002, in press; Rupp, Garcia, & Jamieson, 2001). Variables related most directly to the type and depth of cognitive processing, especially the three variables (a) type of information, (2) type of match, and (3) plausibility of distractors, appear to be most promising for this purpose (e.g., Kirsch & Mosenthal, 1990, 1995; Mosenthal, 1996; see Jamieson et al., 2000).

Many tests of reading comprehension are geared toward assessing a variety of different types of reading comprehension. This approach to test development is the *reader purpose perspective* and is an effective means of communicating to test takers and other stakeholders the design and construct definition of the test. According to Enright et al. (2000), it is useful to coarsely distinguish between four different types of reading comprehension, which entail mental operations of different levels of complexity (pp. 4-5):
1. Reading to find detailed information / search reading,
2. Reading for basic comprehension / main idea,
3. Reading to learn, and
4. Reading to integrate information across texts.

For the design of the standards-based tests at the IQB, a reader purpose perspective was selected as the guiding perspective for test design and test score interpretation in alignment with the types of reading comprehension that are commonly distinguished in other large-scale assessments. However, supplementary information from two types of validation studies is currently being used to strengthen the evidence for the construct validity of the inferences, decisions, and consequences arising from the test scores. First, information about the mental operations that students engage in while responding to items is being gathered via validation studies under a cognitive processing perspective. Second, information about the features of items and their stimulus materials that affect their difficulty is being gathered via validation studies under a reading task perspective and is being collected during item development via classifications of tasks and items by the item writers. However, none of these studies are described in this volume of the technical report series as they will be the subject of separate validation reports.

The Description of Reading Comprehension in the NES and the CEF

Due to its theoretical grounding and practical mandate, the CEF invites a broader definition of the construct of reading comprehension than the NES, which select and adapt pertinent descriptors and types of reading comprehension, texts, and task characteristics from the CEF. Both the CEF and the NES underscore, however, that the language learner is an active language user whose knowledge and skills in multiple languages mutually inform his or her language-based actions. Hence, both documents adopt an *action-oriented approach* towards language use that views members of society as accomplishing meaningful tasks using acts of speech in situations that are part of a relevant social context. Table C1 and table C2 in the appendix list the places in the CEF where scales for specific competency domains can be found while table C3 in the appendix lists the different reading comprehension competencies that are enumerated in the NES.

The competence of reading comprehension is located in the NES within the competency area of *communication skills*, which also includes listening, listening/visual comprehension, speaking, writing, and language mediation. The effective *application of linguistic resources* such as knowledge of vocabulary, grammar, and spelling serves to enhance reading comprehension processes. Furthermore, an effective comprehension of text requires the use of *methodological competencies* such as utilizing a variety of reading strategies that are geared toward comprehending different levels of detail in the text. These can be further supported by marking strategies such as underlining, highlighting, or extracting key words from texts. These strategies can either facilitate or debilitate comprehension processes of the learner depending on the suitability of their application within a given context (see, e.g., Cohen & Upton, 2006; Rupp, Choi, & Ferne, 2006). The strategic use of reference materials such as dictionaries, grammatical resources, or other learning resources can also aid in comprehension processes. Finally, the use of *intercultural competencies* relevant for successful reading comprehension such as the activation of culturally-appropriate schemata and background information can aid performance in reading comprehension depending on the degree of efficiency with which they are applied.

The Construct Definition in the Research Literature

While texts are commonly perceived to be organized sequences of words, modern conceptions of text include *continuous* as well as *non-continuous* texts, the latter of which includes diagrams, charts, pictures, and the like to accommodate a comprehensive notion of reading comprehension as a basic literacy. Almost all research on reading comprehension processes underscores that reading comprehension is *complex, iterative, and integrative* and requires the effective *interaction* of multiple mental components for the creation of multiple mental representations of text. Consequently, there is no such thing as 'the' comprehension of a text.

As Kintsch (1998) noted in his book entitled *Comprehension: A Paradigm for Cognition*,

> "The terms *understanding* and *comprehension* are not scientific terms but are commonsense expressions. As with other such expressions, their meaning is fuzzy and imprecise. [...] What seems most helpful here is to contrast understanding with perception on the one hand and with problem solving on the other." (p. 2)

That is, reading comprehension is more complex than the mere perception and recognition of lines, letters, or word boundaries even though comprehension processes draw upon such perception processes (e.g., Underwood & Batt, 1996; Schnotz & Dutke, 2004; see Neisser, 1994). It is, first and foremost, a *purposeful activity* that shares characteristics with other *problem-solving activities* (e.g., Alderson, 2000; Kobayashi, 2002). While the purpose for reading influences a reader's type of engagement with a text, there are several component processes of reading that are essential for succeeding at almost any purpose of reading that can be imagined. The complexity of the reading comprehension process with respect to these component processes has been echoed over several decades by numerous reading researchers who have shown that an integrated comprehension of a text relies, first and foremost, heavily on their *fluid, accurate, and efficient* application.

In a synthesis of a large body of research on reading comprehension, Carver (1997) proposed a model where reading comprehension is, at its most fundamental level, composed of fluency, word recognition accuracy, and rate of processing, the latter of which might combine processing efficiency and reading rate. Similarly, according to the *verbal efficiency theory* (Perfetti, 1997), a reader is 'proficient' when the component processes of lexical access, propositional encoding, and text modelling are as efficient as possible. Overall, there is ample evidence in the research literature that effective reading comprehension requires *efficient and automatic decoding skills* that are driven by phonological, lexical, and syntactical awareness and decoding abilities, which are facilitated by increased working-memory capacity and processing speed. These capacities, in combination with an efficient application of appropriate *cognitive and meta-cognitive strategies*, further facilitate access to relevant vocabulary and background knowledge that aid in the creation of mental textual representations of different depths and complexities (e.g., Chiappe, Hasher, & Siegel, 2000; Droop & Verhoeven, 1998; Fitzgerald, 1995; Hoien, Lundberg, Stanovich, & Bjaalid, 1995; Lesaux, Rupp, & Siegel, in press; McDugall, Hulme, Ellis, & Monk, 1994; Metsala, Stanovich, & Brown, 1998; Perfetti, 1997, RAND, 2002; Rumelhart, 1994; Schaffner, Schiefele, & Schneider, 2004; Schnotz & Dutke, 2004; Siegel, 1993).

Moreover, recent studies have illuminated how individual differences in the effectiveness of *learning from text* is related to a variety of reader attributes such as characteristics related to his cognitive and psychological makeup (e.g., cognitive ability, intrinsic reading motivation, verbal self-concept associated with reading), characteristics related to the reading task (e.g., background knowledge, thematic interest), and characteristics of his or her familial background (e.g., socio-economic status and education level of parents, social and cultural capital of the family) (e.g., Möller & Schiefele, 2004; Schaffner, Schiefele, & Schneider, 2004). Specifically, there is evidence that cognitive ability and, to a lesser extent, intrinsic motivation, both have strong direct and indirect effects on the success with which learning from text occurs.

Despite the explicit differentiation of various reading tasks and the desired empirical linkage of reader attributes to these tasks, Rost (1991, 1993), on the basis of an extensive synthesis of research, has argued that individual differences in reading comprehension can be best represented by differences on latent variables for *unidimensional psychometric scales*, because subcomponents of reading are often difficult to separate empirically.

Nevertheless, one of the most useful means of discussing individual differences in reading comprehension is to differentiate different levels of mental representation, for which the construction-integration model (e.g., Kintsch, 1998) has proven to be highly useful. The model operationalizes the concept of 'meaning' in texts through *propositions*, which are main idea units generated by the relational properties between nouns, predicates, and modifiers. A strong emphasis in this model is placed on the *interaction between the reader and the text* such that the establishment of an appropriate mental representation of a text cannot be determined on the basis of textual features alone but is dependent on how the reader makes use of them.

The most basic representation of a text is the *surface-level representation* of the text based on the graphemic, lexical, and syntactical properties of the text. While research has provided little evidence that perceptual processes are predictive of individual differences in the surface representation of a text, memory-driven processes such as word recognition through phonological awareness and lexical access help to explain such differences (e.g., Schnotz & Dutke, 2004). At the propositional level, a distinction is made between the *microstructure* of a text, which refers to local propositional arrangements of the text, and the *macrostructure* of a text, which refers to global propositional arrangements of the text derived from the microstructure. That is, both microstructure and macrostructure are the *objective* propositional representations of the text. Orthogonally to them, the theory distinguishes between a *textbase* and a *situation model,* which are different *subjective* propositional representations of the text in the reader's mind. Among the two, the textbase is the exact propositional representation of the text in the reader's mind and the situation model is an augmented propositional representation of the text in the reader's mind. The situation model is created through integrating the propositions from the textbase with propositions from long-term memory based on prior knowledge, imagery, and actions through elaboration and inference processes. Therefore, both surface-level and propositional features of the text can have an impact on how a textbase and a situation model are formed for a specific purpose for reading such as learning from text (e.g., McNamara & Kintsch, 1996).

In other words,

> "neither the micro- nor the macrostructure of the situation model is necessarily the same as the micro- or macrostructure of the textbase, for the reader may deviate from the author's design and restructure a text both locally and globally according to his or her own knowledge and beliefs" (Kintsch, 1998, p. 50).

The impact of text features on comprehension processes, specifically those features that facilitate coherent mental representations of text, is similarly elaborated in the structure-building framework (e.g., Gernsbacher, 1990, 1997). In this framework, comprehension is viewed as a process of building mental representations of text in the form of a nested architecture that consists of the three fundamental processes *activation, enhancement, and suppression*. In short, readers first initiate a mental representation of a text with a first piece of information, which they then develop by mapping incoming information onto the structure – if it is coherent – or by initiating a new substructure – if it is less coherent or unrelated. Comprehension of a text is, thus, fundamentally aided by *coherence cues*, which help readers to map new information onto existing mental structures. Specifically, coherence cues boost the activation of some representations through *enhancement* and dampen the activation of other representations through *suppression*. These processes are viewed in this theory through a neurolinguistic information-processing lens where similar levels of a mental representation are associated with clusters of similarly activated memory cells. In this manner, memory cells can either enhance or suppress the activation level of other cells, the fluidity of which represents the building and rearrangement of mental structures, which similarly requires the *automaticity of lower-level skills*.

The implications of these theoretical results on the component skills and key processes in reading comprehension and the resulting frameworks for higher-order comprehension for the development of the standards-based tests at the IQB are as follows. Most importantly, the level of detail and complexity of the scientific theories of reading comprehension make a direct application to test development impossible. Indeed, it is the *indirect application* of the general principles outlined in these theories that guide the test development process so that interpretations of reading comprehension scores and associated competency levels on the standards-based assessments are commensurate with psycholinguistic models of reading.

Specifically, while all test items require readers to draw on perception skills for reading, care was taken in the design stage to ensure that different items force test-takers to draw on component skills in different combinations and with different levels of complexity. Based on the types of reading comprehension specified in the NES and the associated descriptions of text characteristics in the CEF, texts and questions were designed based on tables of specifications that incorporated key variables reflecting text and task characteristics so that the level of cognitive complexity that is required to solve the comprehension questions was systematically varied across and within targeted proficiency levels. The degree to which this was achieved will need to be evaluated empirically, however, both through post-hoc questionnaires for test-taker strategy use and characteristics as well as verbal-protocol studies (e.g., Ericsson & Simon, 1993; Leighton, 2004).

The Construct Definition in the DESI Study

In DESI, the test design was also grounded in the competency areas of the CEF, but, in contrast to the IQB tests that were aligned with the NES, it was based on extensive curricular content analyses (Nold & Willenberg, 2007). The test design did not explicitly differentiate between different types of reading, but, rather, specified which of the competency areas in the CEF are necessary to respond to a particular type of reading comprehension question; this approach is represented in figure 5.1.

Competences of learners...	help solve...	...tasks that are characterized by...
L	→	Linguistic markers of text segments
L S	→	Decoding of graphemes, words, and structures
L W	→	Focus of item (concrete vs. abstract)
S W	→	Level of comprehension (global vs. detail)
S W	→	Type of information (explicit vs. implicit)

Competences necessary for reading comprehension:

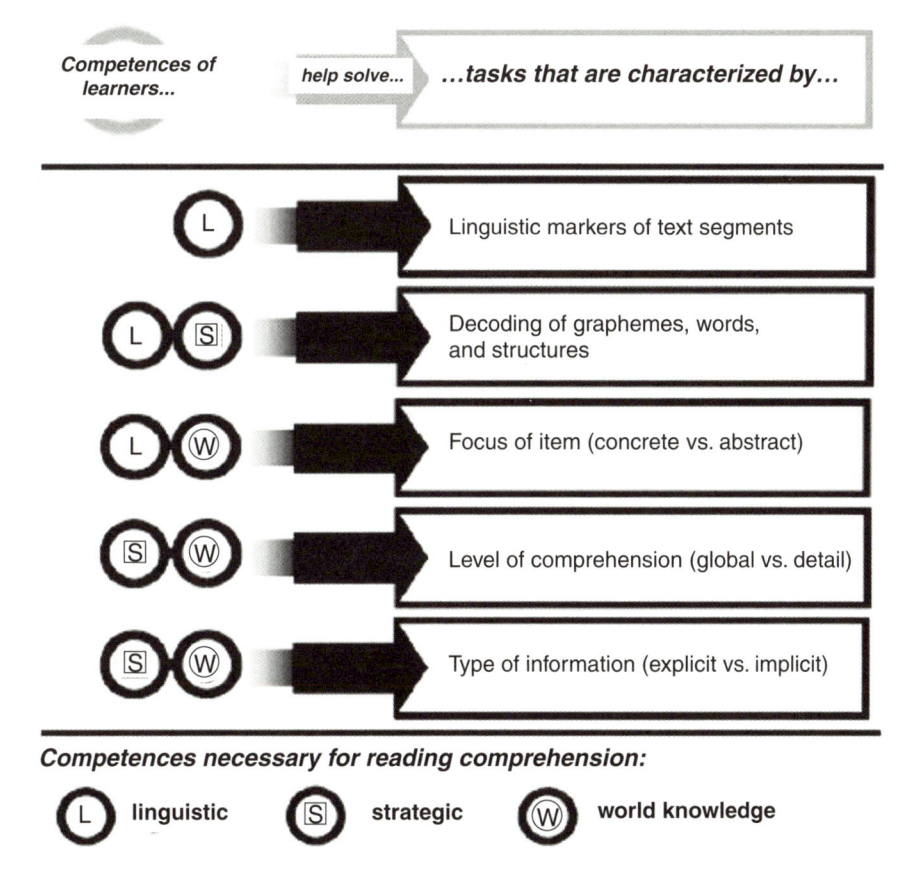

(L) linguistic   (S) strategic   (W) world knowledge

Figure 5.1
Conceptualization of reading comprehension in DESI.

Thus, the DESI study placed a large emphasis on operationalizing the reading comprehension construct through characterizing the cognitive demands of the tasks using potential difficulty features grounded in the CEF (see also section VI of the report).

Operationally, four texts of between 270-400 words each were selected and adapted to represent narrative and informational text types; the test design specifically included a drama text. Each text had 9 to 12 multiple-choice questions associated with it; two texts needed to be solved by each student within 20 minutes. Tasks were classified a priori with the CEF-based *Dutch Grid* (see Alderson & Huhta, 2005; Alderson et al., 2006) by the teachers that developed the items. This classification also led to subsequent psychometric analyses for predicting the empirical difficulty of items that were used as the basis for establishing the cut scores on the proficiency scales. The Dutch Grid was similarly used to train item writers at the IQB, but, in contrast to DESI, this process will be augmented by standard-setting approaches involving different stakeholders (see, e.g., Cizek, Bunch & Koons, 2004; Zieky & Perie, 2006).

In sum, the DESI test, like the standards-based tests developed at the IQB, uses the CEF as a reference for test development and the criteria in the Dutch Grid for classifications of items and the setting of cut-scores to create proficiency levels on the proficiency scales. However, it differs from the IQB tests in that it (a) is based on an explicit match of the test questions with curricula rather than the NES, (b) covers a more restricted range of text types, (c) contains a smaller number of texts, (d) targets a more restricted range of ability, (d) does not explicitly distinguish between different types of reading comprehension, (e) assesses a more restricted range of reading comprehension processes, and (f) does not use consensual standard-setting procedures to augment the psychometric procedures for establishing the proficiency levels of the proficiency scales.

The Construct Definition for the Tests Developed at the IQB

As stated at the outset of this section, the primary guiding documents for developing a construct definition and subsequent test specifications for the tests developed at the IQB are the NES and the CEF. Care was taken in the development of the IQB tasks to utilize authentic materials (see Gilmore, 2007, for a detailed discussion of this term) from the internet or other multi-media sources that contain information and contexts from a variety of cross-culturally relevant situations in different countries in which English is the language of the native speakers (e.g., Great Britain, New Zealand, Ireland, Australia) or one of the official languages (e.g., Canada). Input texts were only minimally modified in selected cases for levels A1 – B1 to match the targeted proficiency level but were generally left as unedited as possible. To avoid cultural biases due to the composition of the ethnic backgrounds of the language learners, demands on intercultural competencies were kept as small as possible by selecting tasks whose contexts would be probably be familiar to the majority of language learners and did not require highly infrequent linguistic or culturally colored material.

Proficiency in basic linguistic skills that facilitate reading comprehension such as knowledge of grammar and vocabulary is not formally assessed even though a certain level of proficiency is assumed for successful performance on tasks targeted at a specific proficiency level. Moreover, the use of methodological competences is partially controlled as no external resources such as dictionaries or notes are allowed during testing. Strategic competences clearly play a role in reading comprehension performance but are not directly assessed. However, information about learning strategies, organization, and awareness are collected via questionnaires from the test-takers and, thus, can be used to analyze the variation in reading comprehension scores.

Based on the formulations for the proficiency levels A1 to C1 in the CEF and the NES as well as the facets just described, the construct of reading comprehension that is assessed by the standards-based tests developed at the IQB is defined as follows:

> *The reading comprehension tests developed at the IQB measure the ability to understand various aspects of continuous and discontinuous written texts as specified in the National Educational Standards for English as a first foreign language (KMK, 2003, 2004) and the Common European Framework of Reference (CEF; Council of Europe, 2001).*
>
> *The texts can be classified as authentic either within or across those cultures where English is spoken as a dominant language, are typical of texts that are valued by these societies, and reflect different narrative and expository genres within these societies. They are typical of texts that need to be comprehended to act competently and autonomously, both within a particular society and across societies to foster the development of plurilingual competencies. Furthermore, they are typical of texts that need to be understood to acquire access to the values and symbols of these societies to foster the development of concurrent pluricultural competences.*
>
> *Their level of difficulty is controlled to elicit reading comprehension performances covering levels A1 to C1 of the CEF. The specific purpose of reading comprehension measured by an individual question or a set of questions tied to a text ranges from understanding specific local details such as disambiguating word meanings to making complex global inferences such as deducing authors' intentions. Therefore, students are required to apply foundational skills of reading and to form mental models of the texts that vary in their level of detail, coherence, and complexity.*

Listening Comprehension

The Assessment of Listening Comprehension in Large-scale Assessments

A variety of factors has been identified that can account for variation in listening comprehension task performance on language assessments (see, e.g., Alderson & Banerjee, 2002; Bejar et al., 2000; Buck, 2001; Freedle & Kostin, 1999; Nissan, deVincenzi, & Tang, 1996). In contrast to reading comprehension assessments, the stimulus for listening comprehension tasks is only acoustically presented reflecting the real-time nature of spoken language. Hence, the unique characteristics of spoken language become particularly important when designing tasks that assess listening comprehension.

Specifically, characteristics of the speakers and their linguistic utterances impact on the degree to which effective listening comprehension can occur in essential ways. For example, age, gender, ethnicity, nationality, occupation, educational level, and first language of speakers influence the manner in which they speak including the structure of their utterances, which often contain several repetitions and redundancies. Relevant aspects of the manner of speech are its rate and clarity, the frequency of pauses and fillers, and the stress and intonation. If multiple speakers are involved, the power relationship amongst the speakers becomes relevant also as it influences the choices of words and structuring of the interaction. Specifically, the speed of turn-taking, the degree of overlap, and the range of accents and dialectal variations are important factors that influence listening comprehension.

Listening comprehension tests also place unique demands on the testing situation. Since a recording is typically used, its quality in terms of the overall loudness and the relative loudness of individual speakers as well as distortions, interferences, and background noise can have significant influence on how the input can be processed by the test-takers. Other factors that influence the difficulty of listening comprehension tasks similar to reading comprehension tasks relate to the nature of the input text itself such as its topic, genre, rhetorical structure, domain, as well as cognitive and experiential demands. Additional important and well-known factors are format effects (e.g., Yi'an, 1998; Shohamy & Inbar, 1991), effects of supplementary visual information (e.g., Ginther, 2001; Gruba, 1997), and effects of prior knowledge (e.g., Jensen & Hansen, 1995; Long, 1990).

Three major approaches to assess listening comprehension are used internationally. First, the *discrete-point approach* focuses on assessing very narrow competences related to isolated linguistic elements such as phonemes, words, or phrases and, hence, is associated with tasks targeting skills such as phonemic discrimination, paraphrase recognition, and response evaluation. Second, the *integrative approach* focuses on the assessment of the mutual execution of various bottom-up skills in conjunction with top-down skills and, hence, is associated with tasks such as gap-filling, dictation, sequence-repetition, statement evaluation, and translations. Third, the *communicative approach* focuses on the assessment of complex integrative skills in a realistic context; tasks under this approach typically utilize authentic input situated within an authentic communicative context and, hence, have an authentic objective. While the discrete point approach has faded in importance over the years, much research has been done on the other two testing approaches. For example, Kaga (1991) and Coniam (1998) investigated the effectiveness of the use of dictation tasks whereas others researched the effectiveness of translation tasks (Stansfield, Scott, & Kenyon, 1990; Stansfield, Wu, & Liu, 1997; Stansfield, Wu, & van der Heide, 2000).

As Buck (2001) notes, however, it is hardly feasible to construct a test that purely measures listening comprehension as tests often require secondary language abilities such as reading comprehension for reading the multiple-choice questions associated with the input or speaking skills if the answer needs to be spoken into a recording device. Researchers such as Henning (1990) have consequently found that such test method effects may contribute to construct-irrelevant variance in the total test score. The influence of test-taking strategies on the test-taker performance for listening comprehension is also being widely researched. For example, Hale and Courtney (1994) examined the effects of note-taking on listening comprehension test performance while Sherman (1997) studied the effects of question preview.

The Description of Listening Comprehension in the NES and the CEF

Due to its theoretical grounding and practical mandate, the CEF allows for a broader definition of the construct of listening comprehension than the NES, which were developed based on selecting pertinent descriptors and types of listening comprehension, text types, and input characteristics from the CEF. Both the CEF and the NES recognize that the language learner is an *active language user*, however, whose knowledge and skills in multiple languages mutually inform his or her language-based actions. Hence, both documents adopt an *action-oriented approach* towards language use that views members of society as accomplishing meaningful tasks using acts of speech in situations that are part of a relevant social context. Just as in the section on reading comprehension, table C1 and table C2 in the appendix list the places in the CEF where scales for specific competency domains can be found. For this subsection, table C5 in the appendix lists the different listening comprehension competencies that are enumerated in the NES.

Listening comprehension is located in the NES within the area of *communication skills*. Listening comprehension, as a receptive communicative activity, involves four main steps, (1) perception of the material, (2) identification of relevant information, (3) connecting this information to form a coherent understanding, and (4) interpretation of this information. These four steps sometimes precede each other in linear sequence in a bottom-up fashion, but are often also reiterated in a top-down fashion. Thus, to fully comprehend aurally presented material, the language user has to be able to successfully *apply linguistic resources* such as auditory phonetic and cognitive skills as well as knowledge of vocabulary, grammar, and pronunciation.

Due to the emphasis of the CEF and the NES on active language use in realistic situations, responding to listening tasks typically requires the skilful application of *intercultural competencies* such as socio-cultural knowledge and intercultural awareness. Apart from intercultural competencies, it is *methodological competencies* as central elements of *functional communicative competence* that the language user typically draws upon when performing listening comprehension tasks (see Goh, 2000). These include general meta-cognitive strategies such as pre-planning, execution, monitoring / evaluation and repair strategies, but also specific listening comprehension strategies that aim at understanding the text at different levels of detail. The CEF describes a range of listening comprehension activities in real-life contexts that require the application of these strategies and provides illustrative scales for these activities (pp. 65-68). Reference materials such as dictionaries, thesauruses, or grammars can further assist listening comprehension for those learners who are skilled in their use.

The Construct Definition in the Research Literature

The research literature on listening comprehension cannot agree on one single definition for a general construct of listening. Nevertheless, a few basic characteristics are widely agreed upon. For example, effective listening comprehension clearly requires an *accurate and efficient decoding* of the aural input since the input is typically not permanently accessible or repeatable as it is part of spoken conversation or monologues that require *immediate and fast real-time processing*.

Consequently, fundamental listening processes involve neurological, linguistic and pragmatic levels of cognition. Listening is bound to the *limited capacity of attention*, which forces the listener to utilize selective attention in his efforts to make sense of the incoming stream(s) of information (e.g., Schmidt, 1995, pp. 20-21). Linguistic processing combines word recognition and parsing to assign semantic roles to words (e.g., Rost, 2002, pp. 20-27). Models of word recognition processes such as the *TRACE* model by McClelland and Elman (1986) and the fuzzy logic model proposed by Massaro (1994) stress the *cyclical and interactive nature of recognition processes* that lead to the activation of words in the mental lexicon. In the light of his knowledge about connected speech patterns, the listener decides which entry in the mental lexicon best matches the string of sounds perceived. Difficulties in processing segments of the linguistic input will often result in a deficit of understanding larger portions of the input such as the main message conveyed in the utterances.

Given the fleeting nature of listening, most research on the psycholinguistic processes in comprehension focuses on reading, which is deemed a less elusive subject matter for empirical research. Studies on listening comprehension thus tend to base their observations on comprehension models that are also employed in analyses of reading, most notably Kintsch's construction-integration model (1998) and Gernsbacher's (1990, 1997) structure-building framework; see the previous subsection on reading comprehension for detailed discussions of these models. Some authors have concluded that the constructs of reading and listening comprehension overlap to a substantial degree in that both receptive skills draw on a similar linguistic and non-linguistic arsenal of competencies and may do so in similar ways (e.g., Bae & Bachman, 1998; Freedle & Kostin, 1999; Grothjahn, 2000; Rupp, Garcia, & Jamieson, 2001).

Similar to reading comprehension, the listener actively constructs meaning by making inferences based on cues that activate linguistic and non-linguistic knowledge. These inferences lead to plausible hypotheses about text meaning and are open to revision upon the encounter of subsequent information. Buck's (1991) introspective study on the testing of second language listening alludes to central ideas in Gernsbacher's work on comprehension by pointing out that "the ability to adjust the interpretation in response to new information is obviously an important listening skill, but especially so in the case of second language listening" (p. 80). Both bottom-up processes and top-down processes interact in this complex process. Bottom-up processes, however, seem to be a stronger determiner of listening performance in a second or foreign language as second or foreign language learners tend to have poorly automatized decoding skills (see Tsui & Fullilove, 1998).

To systematically describe and investigate such component competencies, researchers such as Canale (1983), Canale and Swain (1983), and Bachman and Palmer (1996) have assembled frameworks of *communicative competence* that include listening comprehension as a measurable skill and specifically differentiate between linguistic and strategic competences. Linguistic competences include phonologic, lexical, syntactic, sociolinguistic and pragmatic knowledge as well as knowledge of discourse. Strategic competence refers to information processing and includes cognitive and meta-cognitive strategies to decipher, save and connect linguistic information (see Chapelle, Grabe, & Berns, 1997).

The Construct Definition in the DESI Study

The only major study to date to assess listening comprehension in English as a foreign language in Germany is the DESI study (Beck & Klieme, 2007), which was targeted at 9th graders in the German school system. In DESI, the test design is grounded in the competency areas of the CEF and is based on extensive curricular content analyses (Nold & Rossa, 2007). It adapted the default construct of listening ability from Buck (2001, p. 114), but specifically acknowledged the idea that test-takers typically draw on domain-specific and general world knowledge to successfully construct a mental model of the input in addition to linguistic and strategic competencies. The input selected for the DESI tasks was chosen to align closely with those materials that could be expected in typical school contexts in

Germany, which meant that they tended to be literate and not necessarily authentic in terms of linguistic interactions in everyday contexts by native speakers.

Like the construct definition for reading comprehension, the listening comprehension construct in DESI does not differentiate explicitly between different types of listening, but, rather, specifies, via cognitive task variables, which cognitive operations are necessary to respond to a particular type of listening comprehension question as shown in figure 5.2.

listener's competence **is measured against** variable profiles of task characteristics

- (L) → linguistic characteristics of the input
- (L)(S) → accents, speech rates, articulation
- (L)(W) → concreteness vs. abstractness of content
- (S)(W) → need to understand detail and gist
- (S)(W) → need to recognise, retrieve, infer and interpret explicit and implicit information

(L) language competence   (S) strategic competence   (W) world knowledge

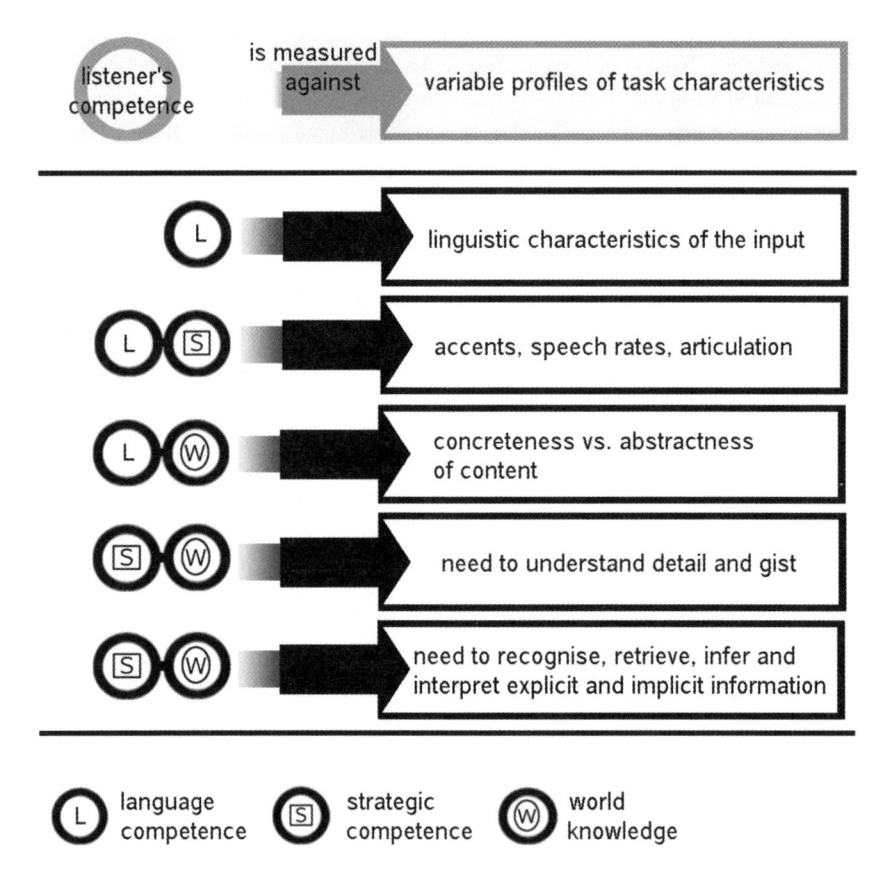

Figure 5.2
Conceptualization of listening comprehension in DESI.

Thus, the DESI study places emphasis on operationalizing the listening comprehension construct through characterizing the cognitive demands of the tasks using potential difficulty features grounded in the CEF and categories identified in research on task difficulty in listening comprehension (see Bejar et al., 2000; Brindley & Slatyer, 2002; Brown, 1995; Buck & Tatsuoka, 1998; Grotjahn, 2000; Henning, 1990; Jensen et al., 1997; Rost, 1990)

Operationally, 16 short dialogues with one multiple-choice item each and four longer texts that resembled radio reports with 7 to 10 multiple-choice items each were used; the dialogues targeted the performance levels A1+ to B1 of the CEF whereas the longer radio reports targeted the levels A2+ to B2+ of the CEF. Tasks were classified a priori with the *Dutch Grid* (see Alderson & Huhta, 2005; Alderson et al., 2006) by the teachers that developed the items. This classification also led to subsequent psychometric analyses for predicting the empirical difficulty of items that were used as the basis for establishing the cut scores on the proficiency scales. For the standards-based tests developed at the IQB, formal consensus-building typical of international standard setting procedures (see, e.g., Cizek, Bunch, & Koons, 2004; Zieky & Perie, 2006) will be used also.

Hence, the DESI test, like the standards-based tests developed at the IQB, uses the CEF as a reference for test development and the criteria in the *Dutch Grid* for classifications of items according to difficulty features and required proficiency level of the student. However, it differs from the IQB tests in that it (a) is based on an explicit match of the test questions with the curricula rather than the NES, (b) covers a more restricted range of text types, (c) contains a smaller number of texts, (d) uses less authentic texts, (e) targets a more restricted range of ability, (f) does not explicitly distinguish between different types of listening comprehension, (g) assesses a more restricted range of listening comprehension processes, and (h) does not use consensual standard-setting procedures to augment the psychometric procedures for establishing the proficiency levels of the proficiency scales.

The Construct Definition for the Tests Developed at the IQB

As stated at the outset of this section, the primary guiding documents for developing a construct definition and subsequent test specifications for the tests developed at the IQB are the NES and the CEF. Information about the difficulty features of the tasks was coded explicitly for each task and its associated items using a detailed grid during the item development process, which was adapted from the *Dutch Grid* and formally summarized in listening test specifications. A professional recording studio was used to improve the quality of the recordings and to record instructions. During test-administration, high-quality players are used in all classrooms and principals have been instructed to reserve classrooms that have good acoustics and as little interfering noise as possible. Recordings are played once or twice depending on the targeted proficiency level and perceived complexity of the input.

Care was taken in the task development process to utilize authentic materials (see Gilmore, 2007, for a detailed discussion of this term) from the internet or other multi-media sources that contain information and contexts from a variety of cross-culturally relevant situations in different countries in which English is either the language of the native speakers (e.g., Great Britain, New Zealand, Ireland, Australia) or one of the official languages (e.g., Canada) or used as *lingua franca*. Input was only minimally modified in selected cases for levels A1 – B1 to match targeted proficiency level but was generally left as unedited as possible. Due to the wide range of materials and topics used, the aim is to wash out differential effects of intercultural competencies on performance.

Proficiency in basic linguistic skills that facilitate listening comprehension such as knowledge of grammar and vocabulary is not formally assessed even though a certain level of proficiency is assumed for successful performance on tasks targeted at a specific proficiency level. Moreover, the use of methodological competences is partially controlled as no external resources such as dictionaries, thesauruses, or notes are allowed during testing. The degree of the successful application of other strategic competencies is not formally assessed, because methods for assessing many of them (e.g., asking the speaker to repeat using a slower rate of speech) are unsuitable for a testing situation. However, information about learning strategies, organization, and awareness are collected via questionnaires from the test-takers and, thus, can be used to analyze the variation in listening comprehension scores.

Based on the formulations for the proficiency levels A1 to C1 in the CEF and the NES as well as the facets just described, the construct of listening comprehension that is assessed by the standards-based tests developed at the IQB is defined as follows:

> *The listening comprehension tests developed at the IQB measure the ability to understand various aspects of spoken text as specified in the National Educational Standards for English as a first foreign language (KMK, 2003, 2004) and the Common European Framework of Reference (CEF; Council of Europe, 2001).*
>
> *The texts can be classified as authentic either within or across those cultures where English is spoken as a dominant language, are typical of texts that are valued by these societies, and reflect different narrative and expository genres within these societies. They are typical of texts that need to be comprehended to act competently and autonomously, both within a particular society and across societies to foster the development of plurilingual competencies. Furthermore, they are typical of texts that need to be understood to acquire access to the values and symbols of these societies to foster the development of concurrent pluricultural competences.*
>
> *Their level of difficulty is controlled to elicit listening comprehension performances covering levels A1 to C1 of the CEF. The specific purpose of listening comprehension measured by an individual question or a set of questions tied to a text ranges from understanding specific local details such as disambiguating word meanings to making complex global inferences such as deducing the intentions of a single speaker or a group of speakers. Therefore, students are required to apply foundational skills of listening and to form mental models of the texts that vary in their level of detail, coherence, and complexity.*

Writing

The Assessment of Writing in Large-scale Assessments

Compared to reading and listening comprehension, fewer large-scale assessment studies exist on testing writing in English as a second or foreign language (for a succinct review of different research traditions in this area and additional citations see, e.g., Alderson & Banerjee, 2002; Wolfe, 2004). Put simply, however, research has shown that it is difficult to develop task prompts that will elicit the sort of written responses that are targeted by the test, to select criteria for the assessment of written responses, and to ensure reliability of rating processes. Researchers and analysts also face economic problems. In order to ensure inter-rater and intra-rater reliability, a rather time-consuming and costly procedure is necessary. Rating scales with labels and descriptors for different analytic criteria need to be developed, benchmark responses representing different skill profiles need to be identified, and raters have to be intensively trained in the use of the criteria with these benchmarks, which makes large-scale studies with lengthy and complex rating schemes prohibitive.

A variety of rating skills for writing exist internationally (see, e.g., Alderson, 1990; North, 2000; Weigle, 2002). Some prominent guidelines for rating writing have been developed by institutions such as *ACTFL* (see the scales in the appendices of the CEF) while others have been developed for specific large-scale assessments such as the TOEFL-iBT, the IELTS exams, or the Cambridge ESOL exams (see section IV of this report). A core characteristic of a *rating* process is that it requires the raters to internally *weight and synthesize* different facets of the written responses to arrive at a particular *analytical criterion score* (e.g., descriptors for 'cohesion', 'coherence', and 'structure' for a criterion called 'organization') or a *holistic score* for the entire response. This is in contrast to *grading* where evaluators are merely asked to indicate whether very specific aspects (e.g., opening and closing statements in a formal letter or an address in an application form) are present in a written response. In large-scale assessments that cover a wide range of proficiency levels both approaches may also be combined in that tasks targeting the lower proficiency levels may result in grading activities whereas tasks targeting higher proficiency levels may result in rating activities.

Rating student responses is a challenging process, however, and *rater training* is geared toward minimizing intra- and inter-individual differences in (a) the *interpretation of descriptors*, which may vary significantly for a particular application (e.g., Lumley, 2002), and (b) the *weighting of different descriptors* to arrive at a composite analytical or holistic rating, which may also vary significantly for a particular application (e.g., Milanovic, Seville, & Shuhong, 1996). A particular problem in this context is the *halo effect*, which refers to the phenomenon that the rating for a particular aspect of the student response unduly dominates the rating of other aspects (e.g., Cumming, 1990; Cumming, Kantor, & Powers, 2001; Kroll, 1998). Before training is implemented the *selection of raters* is a critical issue in this process as they need to have sufficient levels of writing ability in English as well as rational decision-making ability (e.g., Shohamy, Gordon, & Kraemer, 1992).

Once written responses have been rated by human raters it is possible to analyze the resulting data with a measurement model that *corrects the reported scores for the harshness or leniency* of individual raters. Such models are typically *multi-faceted Rasch models* from item response theory (e.g., Embretson & Reise, 2000) and have been applied successfully in large-scale assessments (e.g., Congdon & McQueen, 2000; Eckes, 2005; Weigle, 1999; Wolfe, 2004). An alternative approach that helps to disentangle, but not correct for, different sources of construct-irrelevant variance due to differences in tasks, raters, criteria, learner proficiencies, and their interactions is to conduct a study within the framework of *generalizability theory* (e.g., Brennan, 2001). With such a study it can be determined whether it is advantageous to include more or less tasks, raters, criteria, or learners in a study to obtain targeted *levels of precision* for different types of inferences. This approach has been successfully used in contexts where the rating design was rather simple (e.g., Bock, Brennan, & Muraki, 2000) and where it was as complex as in a typical large-scale assessment (Chiu & Wolfe, 2002). Finally, it should be noted that a growing literature exists on automated scoring of written responses that will not be reviewed here due to (a) space limitations and (b) the fact that the rating of the standards-based writing tasks developed at the IQB will be done with human raters. However, the interested reader is referred to Shermus and Burstein (2003) for an interdisciplinary perspective on this problem and Deane (2006) for a review of some core linguistic challenges in this process.

The Description of Writing in the NES and the CEF

Due to its theoretical grounding and practical mandate, the CEF allows for a broader definition of the construct of writing than the NES, which were developed based on selecting pertinent descriptors and text types in writing from the CEF. Both the CEF and the NES recognize that the language learner is an active language user, however, whose knowledge and skills in multiple languages mutually inform his or her language-based actions. Hence, both documents adopt an action-oriented approach towards language use that views members of society as accomplishing meaningful tasks using acts of speech in situations that are part of a relevant social context. Just as in the section on reading comprehension, table C1 and table C2 in the appendix list the places in the CEF where scales for specific competency domains can be found. For this section, table C6 in the appendix lists the different writing competencies that are enumerated in the NES.

Three competency areas in the first foreign language are distinguished in the NES, which all play an important role for the establishment of effective writing skills. *Communication skills* include writing alongside with reading comprehension, listening comprehension, speaking, and language mediation, all of which depend on the successful *application of linguistic resources* such as knowledge of vocabulary, grammar, and spelling. Furthermore, writing requires *intercultural competencies*, which means, for example, that the learner knows 'rules of communication and interaction' and 'common views and perceptions, prejudices and stereotypes of their own and the foreign culture' as they relate to writing text (KMK, 2004, p. 15). Moreover, *methodological competencies* need to be acquired as another competency area for writing in the first foreign language and include the application of methods to create written texts, the usage of cooperative forms of learning when writing or reviewing text, different learning techniques and strategies like using reference material such as dictionaries and thesauruses as well as the appropriate formatting of written texts.

Written production in the CEF is defined as a productive activity to carry out communicative tasks, which involves the engagement in communicative language activities and the operation of communication strategies. Communication strategies are seen as the application of the meta-cognitive principles of planning, execution, monitoring, and repair action. Specifically, *planning* includes rehearsing, locating resources, considering audience, task adjustment, and message adjustment, which is followed by *execution* that includes compensating, building on previous knowledge, and trying out. Both of these stages are *monitored* to evaluate success so that *repair action* can be taken, which underlines the process character of writing (pp. 57, 63-65). Such a distinction is not made explicitly in the NES; however, part of the methodological competencies, especially the organization of learning and learning awareness, imply that the focus is on the writing process as well as on the writing product. Apart from written production, the CEF gives examples of written mediation like preparing a translation and provides scales for written interaction such as correspondences.

The Construct Definition in the Research Literature

Research in the field of writing is generally divided into four approaches, (1) a focus on the readers and writers emphasizing the *act of writing* as social interaction and construction, (2) a focus on the *product*, (3) a focus on the *processes* during an act of writing, and (4) a focus on the *context* of writing (e.g., Cumming, 1998; Cumming et al., 2000; Hyland, 2002; Polio, 2003). Until the late 1970s research and teaching of written composition has mainly focused on the form of the written product rather than on the process of writing. Beginning in the 1970s, however, composition processes were dissected more closely to develop a psychological model of writing. One very influential model of the writing process, which was modified later by many other researchers, was that of Hayes and Flowers (1980), who highlighted especially that writing is a recursive and not a linear process.

In the cognitive model of Hayes (1996), the task environment and the individual writer were explicitly and carefully distinguished and elaborated on. The *task environment* includes a social component (e.g., the audience, the environment, and other sources that impact the writing process) and the physical component (e.g., the already produced text and the medium with which it is produced), a distinction corroborated by research on differences in the planning and editing processes (see Pennington, 2003). The *individual* factors include motivation and affect, cognitive processes, working-memory capacity, and long-term memory capacity. The model by Hayes (1996) sets itself apart particularly because of its inclusion of the influence of motivational factors on the writing process, which had been previously viewed by many as essential to a successful written communication but not formally included in models of writing. Along similar lines, Weigle (2002) argues that a contemporary model of writing needs to account for the complex interactions between the purpose for which the text is written, the characteristics of the individual writer, the processes during the writing act, the envisioned reader of the text, and the social context in which the writing takes place.

Contextual variables involved in writing are also incorporated in the model by Grabe and Kaplan (1996), which defines the task environment in more detail and includes characteristics of participants, setting, task, text, and topic. This model also differentiates different aspects of *communicative competence / communicative language ability*, namely linguistic, discourse, and sociolinguistic knowledge (e.g., Bachman, 1990; Bachman & Palmer, 1996; Canale & Swain, 1983; Chapelle et al., 1997).

Hayes (1996) also emphasized the necessity of sufficiently developed reading comprehension skills for the production of effective texts and distinguished between reading drafts to evaluate them, reading source texts, and reading instructions. Ideally, of course, reading and writing competencies should be evaluated separately in testing situations to be able to make valid generalizations about learners' abilities in both areas to performance in the target language domain on the basis of the test results. That is, the input of a writing task should not include an extensive reading input or should include only simple instructions whose successful comprehension requires only basic reading skills (e.g., Camp, 1996) unless this is required in the target language situation also.

Many researchers in writing underscore the similarities but also differences of writing in the first and second or foreign language (e.g., Weigle, 2002, Krapels, 1990; Harsch, Neumann, Lehmann, & Schröder, 2007; Grabe & Kaplan, 1996) and the influence of writing competencies in the first language on the acquisition of writing competencies in a second language (e.g., Hyland, 2002). Most of the researchers in that field agree that the main difference for writing is that second language learners have less knowledge about text types and phrases suitable across different situations so that they can rely less on *automatized linguistic skills* such as grammatical or syntactical awareness as well as vocabulary knowledge when solving a writing task. However, many models of the writing process are based on first-language writing and have failed to sufficiently delineate the impact of these facts on the design of writing tasks for a second- or foreign-language assessment (e.g., Hayes 1996; Bereiter, 1980; Bereiter & Scardamalia 1987).

Bereiter (1980), however, takes into account the development of written expression in the foreign language and the limitations students have in their communicative awareness. He differentiates five phases in the development of writing based on the assumption that new skills can only be integrated into a given system if cognitive capacities are available. The first phase, called the *associative phase*, is characterised by the integration of language fluency and ideational fluency. Learners' capacities are occupied with the processing of language so that no capacities are available for planning or taking into account the intended readership. The next phase, called the phase of *performative writing*, focuses on the integration of rules of style and mechanics. That is, learners apply textual, stylistic or orthographic rules with greater care when producing written responses. This stage is followed by the phase of *communicative writing* where social cognition is integrated into the system of writing abilities. Learners in this phase develop awareness of the effects of their writing, of the reader's perspective, or of the necessity to address the target audience. The last two phases, called the phases of *unified* and *epistemic writing*, are characterised by the integration of the skills of critical judgment and reflective thinking. Task and rating scale construction within the domain of writing in a foreign language should take into account those characteristics.

The Construct Definition in the DESI Study

The construct definition of writing in DESI was based on research in text linguistics, language acquisition, and the didactics of writing development as well as an analysis of curricula (Harsch et al., 2007). The *processing model* by Börner (1989), which was based on the Hayes and Flower (1980) model, was used to develop the task characterization and assessment criteria (Harsch, 2006, p. 249-251). Börner regards the process of writing in a foreign language as a dynamic cyclical interaction between teacher, learner and text. He distinguishes two main foci for writing, a *productive mode* focusing on the production of a text and an *intertextual mode* focusing on the revision and continuation of existing texts. The model encompasses three major aspects, *processes* with regard to strategies of planning (i.e., structuring of content and text), phrasing (i.e., grammar, vocabulary, orthography) and revision (i.e., reading and correcting the text), the *environment* (background knowledge, task and writing aids), and the *teaching perspective* (i.e., methods to develop writing skills). While the effects of instructional intervention on the writing proficiency cannot be assessed in product-oriented large-scale studies, the following aspects of Börner's model were used as rating criteria: (a) presentation of content, (b) organization of the text, and (c) correctness and appropriateness of grammar, vocabulary and orthography.

To overcome the discrepancy between 'artificial' writing situations in teaching contexts and 'authentic' writing situations outside of the classroom (see also Gilmore, 2007, for a detailed discussion of this term), the DESI researchers used semi-creative tasks with authentic objectives (i.e., writing a personal letter to a friend or writing a student's report in a school magazine). No assessment of the writing process was undertaken, but the researchers believe that strategies to plan or revise texts were seldom used. Conceptually, Harsch (2007) shows how the potential writing processes were carefully considered in the task design phase by anchoring the construct definition in research on writing acquisition and writing processes.

The Construct Definition for the Tests Developed at the IQB

Within the domain of writing, it was decided not to test certain sub-skills like grammatical competency through separate tests, but, rather, to account for them via analytical ratings. Consequently, the development of tasks for the different levels and the associated rating scales reflect different combinations of demands on those skills. In order to prevent a confounding of reading comprehension and writing abilities, especially for non-native students, the prompts for the tasks were kept as short as possible. Nevertheless, due to the complexity of the tasks at higher levels of difficulty, the prompts were lengthier for those tasks than the prompts for tasks at lower levels of difficulty.

A communicative approach to writing that explicitly states the audience, purpose, and social context of each writing task with a product-orientation was chosen. It should be noted, however, that the survey of the different curricula across the 16 federal states in Germany for the DESI study, which was updated as an external reference point for the test development process at the IQB, showed great variability with regards to the breadth and depth of expected topics, text types, and discourse types covered. The same holds true for school books across Germany. However, it is expected that any construct-irrelevant variance due to knowledge in these areas will be averaged out in aggregated analyses of student performance. The degree to which this holds true needs to be empirically investigated in future validation studies.

The writing tasks represent a *uni-level approach*, which means that the demands in each task prompt regarding text type, communicative functions, and the target audience was tailored so as to elicit a range of written responses corresponding predominantly to what could be expected at one proficiency level. That is, the complexity of the required speech acts and text types and, along with this, the organizational, strategic, and cognitive expectations increase consistently from levels A1 to C1. At level A1, for example, the tasks do not require an organization of a text in coherent paragraphs whereas on the higher levels evidence of various methodological competencies is expected such as the logical development of ideas and the coherent structuring of these ideas in a longer text at level B2. As in DESI, the tasks were developed to be as authentic as possible in terms of topics, rhetorical structures, text types, and discourse features so as to reflect real-life communicative situations.

Moreover, the assessment of the written texts is carried out using analytic rating scales that measure four criteria: *task fulfillment*, *organization*, *grammar* and *vocabulary*. Whereas the descriptors for the criterion *task fulfillment* show minimal variance across the five levels since this variance is provided for by the tasks, the descriptors for the criteria *organization*, *grammar* and *vocabulary* operationalize the increasing and varying demands expected in terms of organizational and language aspects. For each criterion, a three-point graded score (*below / pass / pass plus*) is given, a category for *insufficient evidence* is included, and a holistic score is provided; for more information, please see the rating scales for all proficiency levels in appendix D.

The criteria of the rating scales are based on Bachman's model of communicative competence (Bachman, 1990; Bachman & Palmer, 1996), on the competence models stated in the CEF and the NES, on research in writing assessment (e.g., Alderson, 1990; Brindley, 1998; Hamp-Lyons, 1990, 1996; Lehmann, 1990, 1994; Milanovic, Saville, & Shuhong, 1996; Weigle, 2000), and on approaches taken in other large-scale assessments such as the approach by *Cambridge* as described in Hawkey and Barker (2004), the approach by *Into Europe* as described in Tankó (2005), or the approach by DESI as described in Harsch (2007) and Neumann (2005). Furthermore, the teachers involved in the writing task development were consulted to ensure that the assessment criteria reflect the approaches traditionally taken in German curricula. As North (2000) points out, there are arguments for and against using the same rating categories for different assessment tasks and we refer the interested reader to Fulcher (1995), or Shohamy (1996) for more detailed discussions on this issue. In addition to the development of the tasks and the rating scales, benchmark texts were identified and raters were trained extensively in two one-week workshops on the use of the rating scales using the benchmarks (see also Alderson & Banerjee, 2002; Harsch, 2007; Hyland, 2003; Hamp-Lyons, 1990; Weigle, 2000).

Considering the purpose of the writing test and the logistic necessities of administering and scoring the test, a direct assessment of process variables based on the models discussed in the previous subsections is not possible even though the CEF and the NES view usage of meta-cognitive strategies as crucial for successful written composition. Thus, the effectiveness of writing strategies needs to be examined further in validation studies, which include studies on the longitudinal development of skill and strategy profiles that show the conditions that are necessary for learners to reach the next higher level of writing proficiency on the CEF scale (see also Grabe & Kaplan, 1996, for a summary of research regarding a successful writer).

On the basis of what has been discussed in this section, the construct of the standards-based writing tests developed at the IQB is defined as follows:

The writing tests developed at the IQB measure the ability to produce various types of written texts situated in various socio-cultural contexts for various communicative functions as specified in the National Educational Standards for English as a first foreign language (KMK, 2003, 2004) and the Common European Framework of Reference (CEF; Council of Europe, 2001).

The writing tasks are situated as authentically as possible either within or across those cultures where English is spoken as a dominant language, are typical of situations that are of significance to the students and the target cultures, and reflect different communicative functions relevant for these situations. The tasks are placed in contexts which need to be mastered to act competently and autonomously, both within a particular society and across societies to foster the development of plurilingual competencies.

The level of difficulty is controlled to elicit written performances covering levels A1 to C1 of the CEF. The specific purpose of writing measured by an individual task ranges from producing simple isolated phrases and sentences such as demanded when writing a simple holiday postcard to producing coherent argumentative texts such as an exposition on an abstract topic. Therefore, students are required to apply foundational skills of writing and to produce texts that vary in their level of detail, coherence, and complexity.

Section VI:
Overview of the Item and
Task Development Process

Structure of Item and Task Development Process

All items were developed in a process that lasted from September 2005 to July 2007; table E1 in the appendix shows the timeline for the entire project. The process involved the coordination of work between members of an expert group, item writers in regional groups, and an expert for training and item review, whose roles will be discussed in the following. The core elements of the item development process consisted of the training of item writers, the actual writing of items, the review of items, the pre-trialling and subsequent revision of items, and the release of calibrated items into a final item bank; figure 6.1 shows the basic relationships between these elements. Each of these elements will now be discussed in more detail.

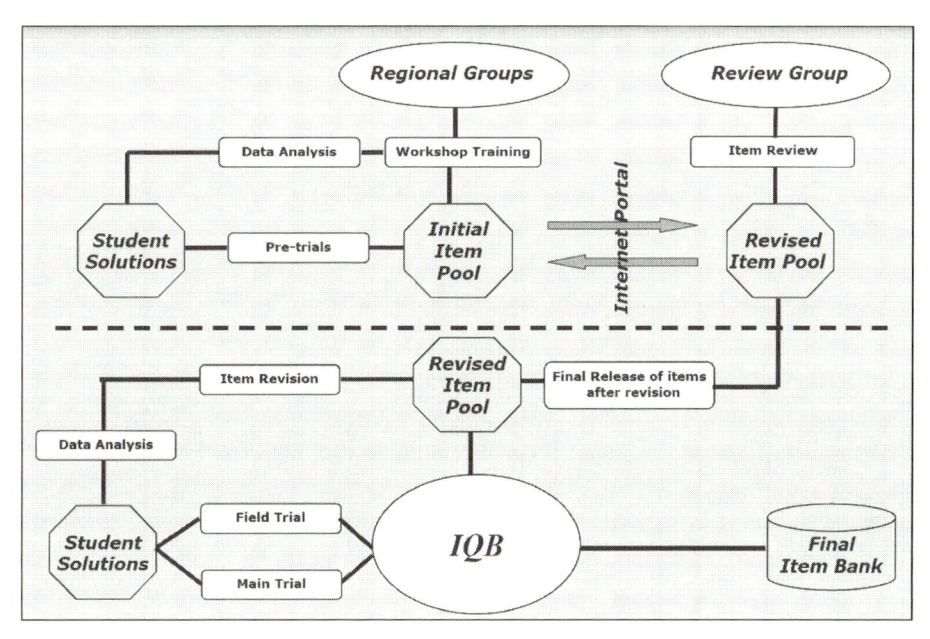

Figure 6.1
Procedural overview of the item and task development process commissioned by the IQB.

In 2005 the KMK selected a number of teachers from the 16 federal states in Germany to participate in the item development process for the standards-based tests at the IQB. The teachers had numerous years of experience in teaching English as a foreign language and, in most cases, experience in curriculum development or the development of standardized achievement tests. The teachers were relieved of a few hours of their weekly workload, but contributed substantial amounts of their personal time to the project on a voluntary basis. As shown in figure 6.2, they worked in four regional groups (north, south, east, and west), which were created based on the geographical location of the schools where they worked to facilitate meetings in person among the regional group members.

81

Expert Group

Coordinator: Dr. Green (Language Testing Consultant, GB)

Dr. Figueras (Generalitat Catalunya, Spain)
Dr. Kaftandjieva (University of Sofia, Bulgaria)
Prof. Dr. Dr. Lehmann (Humboldt University Berlin, Germany)
M.A. Moe (Bergen, Norway)
Prof. Nold (University of Dortmund, Germany)
Prof. Schröder (University of Augsburg, Germany)
Dr. Kecker (TestDaF, Hagen, Germany)
Prof. Dr. Köller (IQB, Berlin, Germany)
Dr. Pant (IQB, Berlin, Germany)
Dr. Harsch (IQB, Berlin, Germany)
Prof. Dr. Rupp (IQB, Berlin, Germany)
Dr. Vock (IQB, Berlin, Germany)

Coordinating Group (Item Development)

Coordinator: Mr. MDgt. Held (Head of School Council of KMK)

Dr. Kindervater (School Council of KMK)
Dr. Kaufmann (Secretary of KMK)
Prof. Dr. Köller (IQB, Berlin)
Ms. Neumann (IQB, Berlin)

Didactic Consulting of Regional Groups
Dr. Harsch
Mr. Rossa

Training of Item Writers
Dr. Green

Regional Group 1 (North)

Coordinator: Ms. Hasche (HH)

NI: Ms. Schuh-Fricke
SH: Ms. Ehlers

Regional Group 2 (West)

Coordinator: Ms. Schmitt-Ford (RP)

BW: Ms. Rehm
NW: Dr. Schier
RP: Mr. Cappel
SL: Ms. Walker-Thielen
    Mr. Leitner

Regional Group 3 (East)

Coordinator: Dr. Nöth (BE)

BE: Ms. McCarthy-Wollenberg
MV: Mr. Hyatt
ST: Ms. Dansokho
BR: Ms. Dornbrach

Regional Group 4 (South)

Coordinator: Ms. Tinis-Faur (BY)

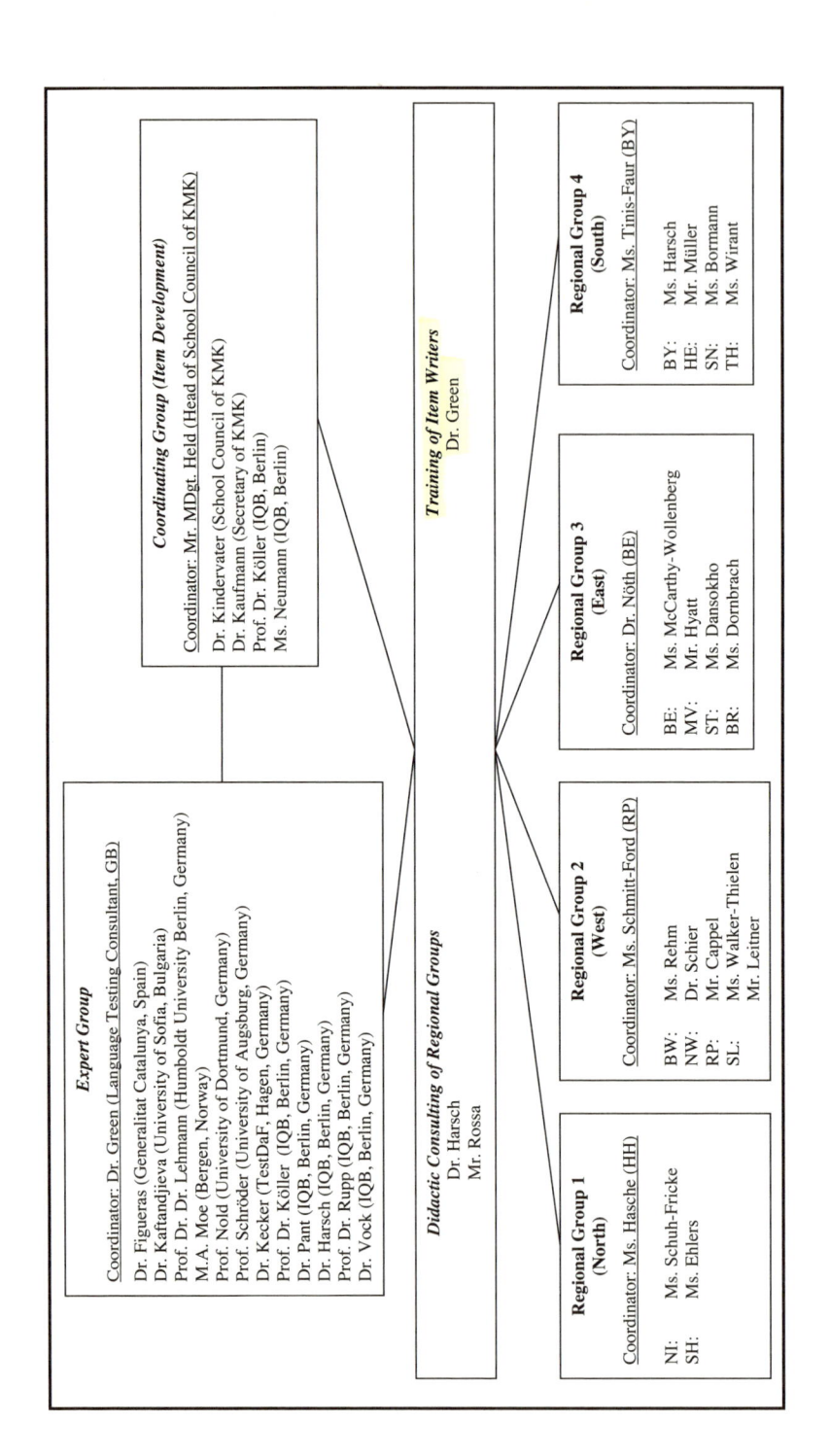

BY: Ms. Harsch
HE: Mr. Müller
SN: Ms. Bormann
TH: Ms. Wirant

Figure 6.2
Organizational structure of the item and task development process at the IQB.

From the beginning of the item development process in October 2005, the teachers were trained regularly in the knowledge and skills of professional item development for standards-based language tests. The training was conducted in nine five-day *workshops* that were held in Berlin or Potsdam for a total amount of 253 hours of training time; see table E2 in the appendix for the schedule and activities of the workshops. The workshops were facilitated by Dr. Rita Green, an internationally renowned expert in language test development who provided many opportunities for practical exercises and peer discussion. In addition, the item development process was frequently reviewed by an international expert team, which met regularly in Berlin (see figure 6.2).

The workshops were sequenced in such a way that each workshop focused on the competence for which test items were to be developed at the time. Specifically, item writers were first charged with developing items for reading comprehension, then with developing items for listening comprehension, then with developing tasks for writing, and finally with tasks for speaking; the speaking tasks were not included in the field and main trials, however, and are not discussed in detail in this technical report. Despite this seemingly linear progression, the process of item and task development was actually highly iterative and caused the item writers to be working on different items and tasks at the same time.

The items and tasks were developed independently by the teachers following each workshop and were uploaded to a portal at the IQB via a secure website. To perform the upload, the teachers used a Microsoft Word template, which required them to classify the texts and associated items for the reading and listening comprehension tasks as well as the writing and speaking tasks according to a variety of relevant criteria for language test development adapted from the *Dutch Grid* (see Alderson & Huhta, 2005; Alderson et al., 2006). These criteria included, but were not limited to, the types of texts / recordings that were used as input or were to be produced, the types of reading comprehension, listening comprehension, writing, or speaking skills that were assessed by each task and / or item and the perceived difficulty level of both the input as well as the item and / or task; see appendix F for the reading and listening comprehension criteria.

The items and tasks were subsequently reviewed first by other item writers within the team and then by Dr. Green according to commonly accepted criteria for quality control in language test development. Consequently, Dr. Green released the items and tasks for future use, requested their revision, or eliminated them from the set of items available for future use. In the case of necessary revisions, each item and task was again reviewed by Dr. Green until it was finally released into a secure item bank. Once a suitable number of released items and tasks for a particular competence had been amassed, they were assembled into booklets and pre-trialed using standardized conditions and instructions.

Several *pre-trials* were used for the items and tasks for each language skill, which are described in more detail in section VII of this report. They consisted of small-scale standardized trials whereby the teachers that had developed the items administered them in their own classes or classes of colleagues; the responses were graded by the teachers at regional group meetings; table E3 in the appendix presents the sample characteristics of the pre-trials. The primary objective of these trials was to identify grossly malfunctioning items, tasks, and distractors, problems with the instructions, problems with the texts and recordings, or difficulties with the estimated response times for each item or task; table E4 in the appendix presents basic psychometric characteristics of the items in the pre-trials for reading and listening comprehension as well as writing. Furthermore, the effects of motivation, familiarity, and ability on the computation of item and task characteristics were investigated.

The results of the pre-trials were discussed in subsequent workshops to identify areas of concern so as to optimize the item development process. Dr. Green explained and discussed the empirical information concerning the performance of each item to the item writers in the workshops, which included statistics from classical test theory such as item difficulty, item discrimination, percent of students selecting each distractor, and Cronbach's α. Furthermore, Dr. Green discussed the feedback from the test takers as well as their relevant background characteristics, and what insights these provided with regards to the performance of the items / tasks. As a result of the trials, items and tasks were again reviewed by Dr. Green and either released for further use, tagged for revision, or excluded from further use. A final set of items and tasks was then released for use in the *field trial* in 2007.

The development processes of listening and reading comprehension items focused predominantly on the selection and modification of appropriate stimulus texts, the creation and revision of items appropriate to each proficiency level, and the development of standardized coding instructions for constructed responses. The development of writing tasks focused more heavily on the development of prompts that would elicit a targeted range of written responses as well as the development of rating scales and rating procedures. This was an iterative process that involved the analysis and adaptation of pre-existing assessment scales along with the creation of descriptors suitable to the specific writing tasks. The development of the rating scales was grounded in the following key documents:

- Relevant illustrative scales from the CEF (pp. 61 and pp. 82 for written production and interaction, pp. 109 for language competencies)
- The *Written Assessment Criteria Grid* from the *Manual* (Council of Europe, 2003, p. 82)
- Rating scales from the DESI project (Harsch, 2007)
- Rating scales from the Hungarian project *Into Europe* (Tankó, 2005)

The writing tasks were rated holistically as well as analytically according to four criteria (i.e. *task fulfillment, organization, grammar* and *vocabulary*), which were derived from these documents and from the construct definition as outlined in section V in this report. These documents also served as a starting point for the selection of preliminary descriptors for each of the four analytical criteria. The rating scales were trialed by the teachers in one five-day workshop to familiarize them with the scoring concept and the assessment instrument. The teachers then applied the scales to performances stemming from a writing pre-trial where they scored a total of 910 scripts based on 23 tasks ranging from A1 to B1 by using an approach in which each script was rated by two independent raters. The analysis of these data as well as the feedback from the teachers resulted in necessary revision of the writing tasks and the rating descriptors.

At the time of the publication of this report, between September 2005 and July 2007, the item writers had developed a total of 551 reading comprehension items associated with 99 tasks or testlets, 429 listening comprehension items associated with 78 tasks or testlets, and 86 writing tasks. At the time of publication of this report, the field trial was underway. In the field trial, 393 reading comprehension items associated with 71 tasks or testlets, 352 listening comprehension items associated with 65 tasks or testlets, and 19 writing prompts were utilized corresponding to 71.32%, 82.05%, and 22.09% of the released items in the item pool.

Composition of Expert Group

To discuss, plan, and adjust the overall test development process, an international expert group was assembled, which met four times between September 2005 and March 2007 (see table E1). The results of the expert meetings had an influence on the strategies that were adopted concerning item development, test administration, the linking of scales with the CEF, and standard-setting.

As shown in figure 6.2, the expert group consisted of Dr. Rita Green (Language Testing Consultant, Great Britain), Dr. Felianka Kaftandjieva (University of Sofia, Bulgaria), Dr. Neus Figueras (Generalitat Catalunya, Spain), Prof. Dr. Dr. Rainer Lehmann (Humboldt University Berlin, Germany), Eli Moe (Bergen, Norway), Prof. Dr. Günter Nold (University of Dortmund, Germany), Prof. Dr. Konrad Schröder (University of Augsburg, Germany), Dr. Claudia Harsch (University of Augsburg, Germany, now IQB), Dr. Gabriele Kecker (TestDaF, Hagen, Germany), Prof. Dr. Olaf Köller (IQB), Prof. Dr. André A. Rupp (IQB), Dr. Anand Pant (IQB), and Dr. Miriam Vock (IQB). The members that were external to the IQB were selected based on their experience with the development of large-scale assessments, the linking of assessments with the CEF, the conduct of standard-setting processes, the methodological design for the collection and psychometric analysis of test data, and the communication of test results to stakeholders within the German educational and political system.

Profile of Trainer and Workshops

Each workshop was facilitated by Dr. Rita Green, an internationally renowned expert in the field of language test development. After several years of work in the field of language testing, Dr. Green received an M.A. in Teaching English as a Foreign Language at the University of Lancaster where she wrote her thesis on parallel tests. After eight more years of practical language testing experience in projects overseas, she received her Ph.D. in Language Testing from the University of Reading where her doctoral work focused on an investigation into the componentiality of academic reading and listening skills.

Dr. Green has been involved in a range of projects in many different parts of the world with organizations such as the British Council / Department for International Development since the early 1990s, the British Ministry of Defence between 2001 and 2005, as well as EUROCONTROL between 2004 and 2007. She provides seminars in language test development in a range of countries such as Austria, France, Italy, Lithuania, Spain, the UK, and Uzbekistan. Since 2001 Dr. Green instructs her own course in language testing at Lancaster University (*Language Testing at Lancaster*) and regularly presents her work at conferences such as the Language Testing Forum, the Language Testing Research Colloquium, EALTA and conferences funded by the British Council.

Her didactic approach for all the workshops centered on an active participation of the item writers. Hence, apart from an initial grounding in the theory of each skill, most of the seminar time was devoted to discussions and pair- or small-group work. The objectives of the workshops were (1) to familiarize the item writers with the CEF, NES, Dutch Grid, and other test development frameworks, (2) to provide them with information about key concepts and processes in language test development so as to sensitize them to critical issues, (3) to allow for numerous practical experiences with the development of items and tasks, test specifications, and test materials, and (4) to empower them to transfer this knowledge to their own item-writing contexts outside of the workshops. That is, the item writers were trained to become experts in the item writing process with the role of Dr. Green being more of a facilitator than an instructor.

Section VII:
Preliminary Empirical Investigations of Items and Tasks

Pre-trials of Reading and Listening Comprehension Tasks

The pre-trials for reading and listening comprehension were small scale standardized trials that used a convenience sample of classes that were located in the schools where the item writers taught at the time. Consequently, the pre-trials were administered and scored by the teachers themselves using standardized instructions and scoring guides.

There were two pre-trials for these skill areas. The first pre-trial included tasks targeting proficiency levels A2 and B1, which were of central interest for operationalizing the *National Educational Standards (NES)* (KMK, 2003, 2004) while the second pre-trial included tasks targeting all five proficiency levels that are included on the standards-based tests developed at the IQB (i.e., proficiency levels A1 to C1). As shown in table E3 in the appendix, all pre-trial samples included students from throughout Germany, both grades 9 and 10, and all four major school types (*Hauptschule, Realschule, Gesamtschule, Gymnasium*); only the first listening pre-trial did not include students from the *Gesamtschule*.

The test booklets were prepared by Dr. Green and photocopied at the IQB. They were either sent via registered couriers to the schools where the item writers worked 3-5 days before the pre-trial dates or were carried to the testing site by an IQB employee at the days of testing. All test administration and scoring procedures as well as data-collection instruments were standardized during the training workshops including the feedback questionnaires; see appendix G for the reading, listening, and writing questionnaires. Student responses were scored by the teachers in their regional groups using anonymous student IDs and submitted to the IQB where the scores were entered, cleaned, and prepared for data analysis by IQB staff and Dr. Green.

Between 324 and 565 students participated in each of the four pre-trials where between 16 and 20 tasks corresponding to between 96 and 124 items were empirically tested. As the results of the pre-trials in table E4 in the appendix show, the internal consistency estimates for the different test forms utilized in the pre-trials ranged from .76 to .90 ($M = .83$, $SD = .05$) and provided first pieces of empirical evidence that the test forms measured homogeneous constructs. Nevertheless, it needs to be kept in mind that the students in the convenience samples were expected to be more motivated and more familiar with the testing formats and objectives than students in a truly random sample.

Extra Trials of Reading and Listening Comprehension Tasks

To obtain supplementary information about the external as well as the generalizability aspects of the construct validity of the reading and listening comprehension tasks, two extra trials were conducted. The first extra trial took place in July 2006 and involved 651 students (53% girls) from the states of Baden-Wurttemberg and Bavaria, which are states with generally high-achieving student populations. A total of 24 classes was sampled with eight classes ($n = 195$)

belonging to the *Hauptschule* (i.e., with students targeting a *Hauptschulabschluss*), eight classes (*n* = 229) belonging to the *Realschule* (i.e., with students targeting predominantly a *Mittlerer Schulabschluss*), and eight classes (*n* = 227) belonging to the *Gymnansium* (i.e., with students targeting predominantly an *Abitur*). Of those students, 476 students were assessed again in January 2007 during the second extra trial to obtain some information about the stability of item and task characteristics over time.

The students were administered reading comprehension tasks during the first extra trial and listening comprehension tasks during the second extra trial. The tasks targeted proficiency levels A1-C1 with tasks targeting proficiency levels A1-B2 administered to students in *Hauptschule* and tasks targeting proficiency levels A2-C1 administered to students in *Realschule* and *Gymnasium* due to expected floor effects in performance. In addition, a C-test (e.g., Eckes & Grotjahn, 2006) measuring overall language ability, reading and listening comprehension tests from the DESI study (e.g., Beck & Klieme, 2007), and a reading section from the short form of the TOEFL test (Educational Testing Service, 2000) were administered. Finally, the most recent school grades in mathematics, German, and English were collected. The results from the extra trials showed correlation patterns between scores that were in the expected directions; table 7.1 summarizes the results.

Table 7.1
Correlation Patterns for Extra Trials

	Tests			Grades		
	C-Test	DESI	TOEFL	Math	German	English
Reading Comprehension	.88	.87	.81	-.20	-.31	-.43
Listening Comprehension	.80	.93	.65	-.13	-.19	-.39

Notes. All variables are correlations for latent variables. Negative correlations are a result of the negative ordering of German school grades with '1' corresponding to an 'A' (i.e., best possible grade) and '6' corresponding to an 'F' (i.e., worst possible grade).

Table 7.1 shows that there is a strong relationship between the IQB test scores and general C-Test and DESI scores, the latter of which also target school-age populations. There is a moderate to strong relationship between the IQB test scores and the test scores from the TOEFL, which targets a more academically-oriented adult population. Moreover, correlations between the IQB test scores and English grades were moderate, correlations between the IQB test scores and German grades were slightly lower, and correlations between the IQB test scores and mathematics grades were weakest, which is conceptually desirable.

The extra trials also provided preliminary evidence that the *a priori classifications* of the tasks and items into CEF proficiency levels by the item developers worked well for reading comprehension and moderately well for listening comprehension; figure 7.1 shows the relationships between the classifications and the empirical difficulty values for reading and listening comprehension tasks.

Specifically, more than half of the observed variation in the empirical item difficulties of the reading tasks could be accounted for by the *a priori* proficiency level ratings ($\eta^2 = .55$). Hence, tasks targeted at a lower proficiency level (e.g., A1) are generally associated with lower item difficulty values (i.e., with easier items) while tasks targeted at a higher proficiency level (e.g., C1) are generally associated with higher item difficulty values (i.e., with more difficult items). However, the predictive power of the *a priori* ratings was lower for the listening comprehension tasks ($\eta^2 = .34$).

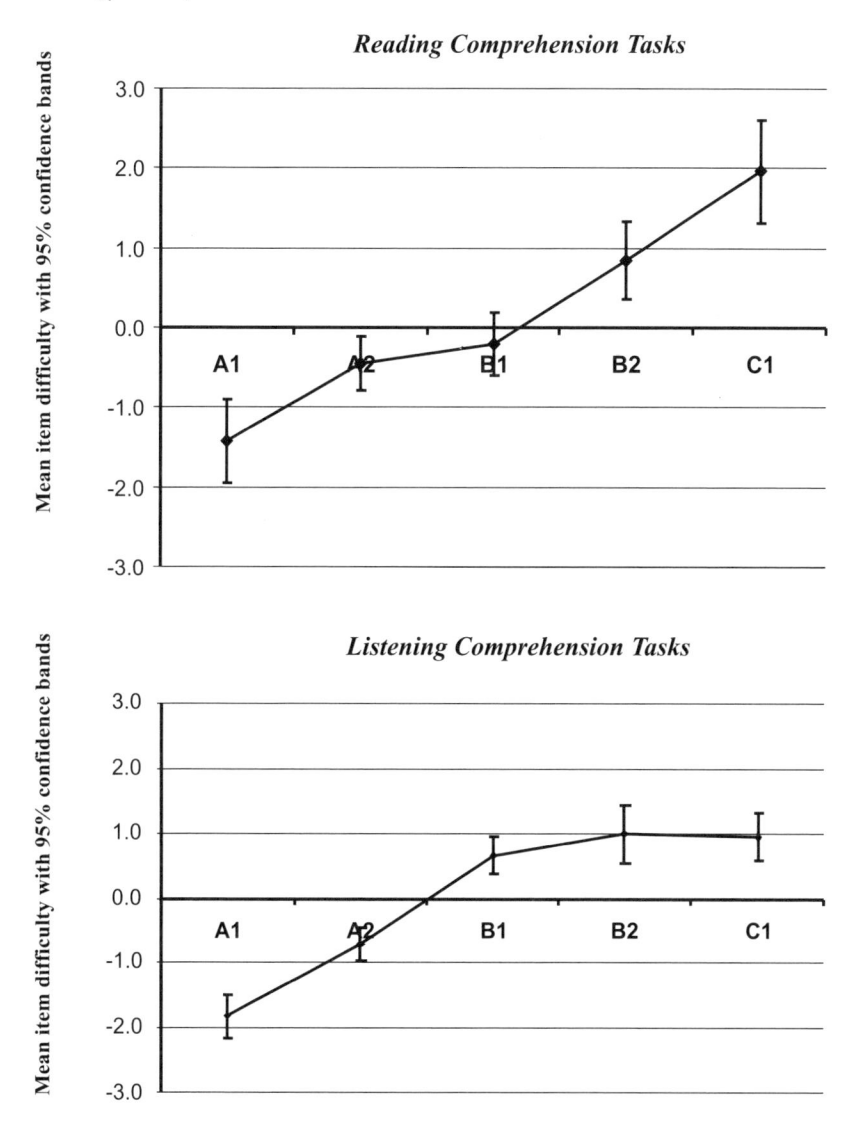

Figure 7.1
Relationships between target proficiency level and empirical item difficulty.

As is also apparent from figure 7.1, a priori classifications and empirical difficulty values alone are not sufficient to set cut-scores on the reading proficiency scale as there is a large degree of overlap between the item difficulty distributions in proficiency levels A2 and B1 for the reading comprehension tasks, which are most important for making policy decisions based on the NES, as well as for levels B1 to C1 for the listening comprehension tasks.

In sum, the extra trials provided preliminary evidence that the item development process was generally functioning effectively but also corroborated the need for more advanced psychometric and consensual approaches to the setting of cut-scores following the field and main trials.

Pre-trial of Writing Tasks

The writing pre-trial took place in January 2007 and was administered to 8th, 9th, and 10th graders at the *Hauptschule, Realschule,* and *Gesamtschule*. A total of 36 tasks covering proficiency levels A1 to C1 were compiled into 12 booklets. However, only the responses of $n = 468$ 9th and 10th graders (50% boys) for 20 tasks had been rated at the time of publication of this report due to time constraints; the rating was done by the item developers after one week of training in using the analytical rating scales.

There were three principal purposes of the pre-trial. First, the empirical parameters of the writing tasks needed to be established and the a priori classification of the tasks according to the proficiency levels needed to be compared with the breadth of student solutions elicited. Second, feedback was needed on the clarity and usability of the rating scales. Third, benchmarks needed to be identified so that they could be used for future training sessions, especially those for the field and main trials. The identification of benchmarks was coordinated by Dr. Green and took place during the following workshop in cooperation with the item developers.

All tasks were rated by two raters who rated between 9 and 63 student responses for each task for a total of $n = 756$ responses; table 7.2 shows the results.

Table 7.2
Range of Percent Agreement for Tasks at Different Levels

Level	# Tasks	% Agreement (Minimum)	% Agreement (Maximum)	# Responses (Minimum)	# Responses (Maximum)
A1	4	38.0	71.4	21	43
A2	2	70.6	75.5	52	55
B1	11	50.0	78.4	9	63
B2	3	16.0	80.5	23	49

Clearly, the range of percent agreement for tasks at different levels was rather wide ($M = 63.8\%$) indicating that the ratings for some tasks worked well whereas ratings for other tasks needed improvement. The results from the pre-trial thus helped to empirically pinpoint those tasks whose prompts needed to be modified and for whom additional student responses needed to be identified that could serve as benchmarks for additional rater training.

Extra Trial of Writing tasks

To obtain supplementary information about external validity aspects and to compare the *uni-level rating* approach followed by the IQB with a *multi-level rating* approach used in the DESI study, an extra trial for the writing tasks was conducted during April and May 2007 at 10 *Gymnasium* schools in Berlin. The student responses for the DESI task could be placed at any proficiency level between A1 and B2+/C1 based on holistic and analytic ratings. The motivation for using *Gymnasium* schools was to overcome the primary limitation of the pre-trial of the writing tasks, which used a student population whose overall ability level was too low to gain insight into the performance of the writing tasks at levels B2 and C1.

Specifically, five B2 and five C1 tasks from the IQB task pool were administered along with four DESI tasks to $n = 400$ 12th graders. The students attended 12 lower-level English courses with two hours of English instruction per week and 10 higher-level English courses with five hours instruction per week. Each student worked on three writing tasks, one IQB task at level B2, one IQB task at level C1, and one task from the DESI project. The tasks were compiled into 10 preliminary booklets. Each booklet contained three tasks to allow for a linking of the students and tasks across the different booklets. In order to avoid order effects, the DESI-task either appeared at the beginning or at the end of each booklet resulting in 20 final booklets altogether. The student responses from the IQB-tasks were rated by two randomly selected item developers while the student responses from the DESI-tasks were rated by trained teacher education students.

The inter-rater agreement of the IQB tasks as measured by Cronbach's α ranged from .47 to .94 for the holistic rating whereas the inter-rater agreement for the holistic rating of the two DESI-tasks was .75 and .78; the results for the holistic and five analytical rating categories are shown in table 7.3. These results provided some evidence that both rating approaches could lead to comparable levels of inter-rater agreement. However, the wider range of the inter-rater agreement coefficients for the uni-level tasks revealed difficulties with individual tasks despite some evidence for a comparable functioning for other tasks.

Table 7.3
Inter-rater Reliabilities

	IQB Tasks Level B2 (k = 5)	IQB Tasks Level C1 (k = 5)	DESI Tasks (k = 2)
Global	.47 to .77	.63 to .94	.75 to .78
Content	.45 to .72	.40 to .97	.82 to .84
Organization	.29 to .54	.39 to 1.0	.70 to .70
Vocabulary	.47 to .74	.31 to .91	.73 to .82
Grammar	.35 to .72	.61 to 1.0	.74 to .76

By using both the IQB and the DESI tasks it was also investigated whether classifications arising from the different tasks and rating approaches are consistent. For example, one would expect that students that were classified as *below* on an IQB task at level B2 should be classified as being at levels A1 to B1 on a DESI task. As the results in table 7.4 for the B2 task demonstrate, a relatively high level of consistency was reached with both rating approaches leading to an agreement in 66.0% of the cases (i.e. the sum of the *italicized entries*) for this task. Almost all of the remaining cases of disagreement differ by at most one competency level.

Table 7.4
Agreement of Holistic Ratings from the Uni-level and Multi-level Approaches for B2 Task

Multi-level Rating	Uni-level Rating		
	Below	Pass	Pass Plus
A1	*0.7*	0.7	---
A2	*3.9*	0.7	---
B1	*33.3*	14.4	---
B2	11.8	*28.1*	2.0
C1	---	4.6	---

Note. Italicized entries signal agreement.

It was investigated next whether the analytical ratings reflected performance on one writing dimension by fitting an exploratory one-factor model to the rating data. Figure 7.2 shows the model for the IQB tasks at level B2 as well as the DESI task. The model shows clearly that the ratings can be well summarized by a common latent factor with all analytical ratings providing very similar levels of information for it.

Furthermore, the latent factor is highly correlated with the global rating providing evidence that the global rating indeed captures most of the information that is contained in the separate analytical ratings. Specifically, 82% of the observed variance on the IQB task at level B2 can be accounted for by the variation in the rating factor while this is true for 88% of the observed variance on the DESI task. Thus, these results provide further evidence that the rating approach is, overall, working the way it was intended.

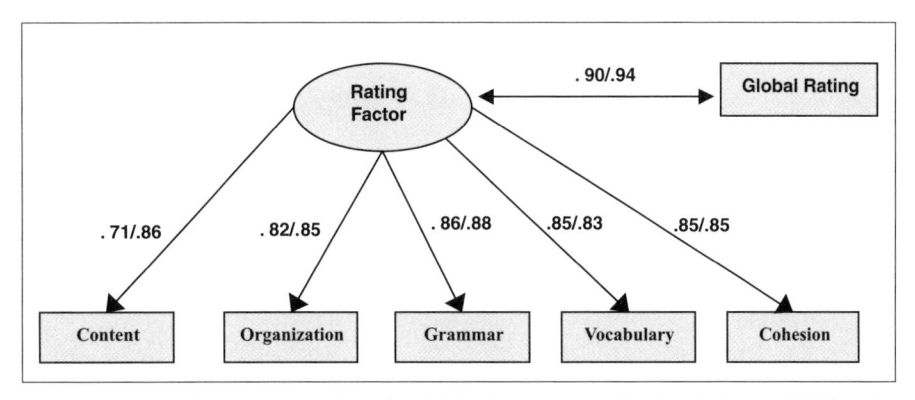

First number indicates IQB tasks at level B2 whereas second value indicates DESI task.

Figure 7.2
Factor model for analytical and holistic ratings.

Finally, school grades in German, English, and mathematics were collected and correlated with the proficiency level classifications and performance differences for students of different sexes and from different course types were computed; table 7.5 shows illustrative results for one IQB task at level B2.

Table 7.5
Performance Difference on IQB Task at Level B2

Rating	BC	AC	d	$p < .05$	Male	Female	d	$p < .05$
Global	1.40	1.77	.77	✓	1.55	1.57	.05	
Content	1.76	1.96	.46	✓	1.76	1.91	.31	✓
Organization	1.48	1.79	.71	✓	1.56	1.64	.18	
Vocabulary	1.41	1.79	.75	✓	1.57	1.56	.02	
Grammar	1.33	1.62	.59	✓	1.44	1.46	.03	
# Ratings	200	142	---	---	144	197	---	---

Note. BC = Basic course with two hours of instruction per week, AC = advanced course with five hours of instruction per week.

The ratings for the task were coded trichotomously (1 = *below*, 2 = *pass*, 3 = *pass plus*) so that d represents the standardized mean difference in ratings using the pooled standard deviation. As expected, students in advanced courses outperform students in basic courses, on average, on all rating criteria whereas girls only outperform boys on *content* and, even though not statistically significant, show superior performance on *organization* as well. These results illustrate the generally satisfactory functioning of this IQB task and such analyses will have to be repeated for all writing tasks during the field trial.

Feasibility Study of Writing Tasks

In May 2007, a feasibility study was launched in cooperation with the *Data Processing Centre* in Hamburg to examine how the uni-level rating approach could be practically implemented on a large scale for the field trial. Specifically, the study was used to obtain additional information on the general functioning of the uni-level rating approach, on the interpretation of the rating scale descriptors, on the adequacy of handbooks developed to guide the rating procedure, on the benchmarks that are used during rater training, and on the rating software that is used for this process by the DPC.

In this study, two IQB tasks at levels A2 and B1 were rated by six teacher education students. The students were selected based on several measures of their English proficiency generally and their writing proficiency more specifically to control for effects of ability differences on the rating outcomes. The raters were familiarized with the rating approach, the writing tasks, the rating handbooks, the benchmarks, and the software during an introductory one-day training session. During the week after the introductory training, the raters practiced on 25 student responses per writing task and rated each response on five criteria (i.e., the three-point holistic rating as well as the four three-point analytic ratings for *task fulfilment, organization, grammar,* and *vocabulary*). In a follow-up training session, raters received feedback on their levels of agreement, and reasons for discrepancies in the ratings were discussed. After this second training session, raters rated another 30 student responses per writing task.

The following data are based on the set of ratings that were collected after the second training session. Table 7.6 shows the degree of inter-rater agreement aggregated over all ratings, once over both tasks and once for each task separately. The results show that 44.4% of ratings were exactly identical for both tasks and that 71.3% of the ratings differed by at most one point.

Table 7.6
Inter-rater Agreement for Two IQB Tasks in Feasibility Study

Both Tasks

# of Valid Ratings (n = 275)	% Agreement	Total Agreement
26	9.5	3 out of 6
53	19.3	4 out of 6
74	26.9	5 out of 6
122	44.4	6 out of 6

B1 Task

# of Valid Ratings (n = 135)	% Agreement	Total Agreement
15	11.1	3 out of 6
23	17.0	4 out of 6
41	30.4	5 out of 6
56	41.5	6 out of 6

A2 Task

# of Valid Ratings (n = 140)	% Agreement	Total Agreement
11	7.9	3 out of 6
30	21.4	4 out of 6
33	23.6	5 out of 6
66	47.1	6 out of 6

Utilizing the modal rating that was provided by the raters for the student responses associated with a task, the percent agreement with the modal category was computed for each rater as an estimate of their intra-rater reliability.

Table 7.7
Intra-rater Reliabilities for Two IQB Tasks in Feasibility Study

Criterion	Rater 1	Rater 2	Rater 3	Rater 4	Rater 5	Rater 6
A2 Task						
Task Fulfilment	.82	.78	.70	.74	.70	.82
Organization	.89	.96	.70	.85	.78	.93
Grammar	.78	.96	.74	.82	.85	.93
Vocabulary	.82	.96	.70	.85	.93	.96
Holistic Rating	.85	1.00	.74	.89	.70	.96
B1 Task						
Task Fulfilment	.93	.86	.79	.89	.68	.89
Organization	.86	.93	.79	.93	.71	.96
Grammar	.89	.96	.82	.61	.86	.93
Vocabulary	.79	.96	.93	.82	.79	.93
Holistic Rating	.86	.93	.79	.86	.57	1.00
Mean	.93	.86	.79	.89	.68	.89

As table 7.7 shows, the reliability values ranged between .57 and 1.00 overall, the mean reliability for each rater ranged from .76 to .93 indicating satisfactory rating performance of the six raters. Similarly, the inter-rater reliabilities for each analytical criterion were sufficiently high as they ranged from .76 to .87 across the two tasks.

In brief, the results of the feasibility study provided detailed qualitative information that helped to improve the training materials as well as quantitative information that supported a reliable use of the uni-level rating approach on a large scale. With the information from the pre-trial, the extra trial, and the feasibility study, the rating approach will be fine-tuned for the field and main trials. For the field trial, rater training will take place during July and August 2007 where 15 raters will be trained over a period of 6 weeks to rate the 19 tasks at levels A1 to C1.

Section VIII:
Characteristics of Tasks in the Field Trial Pool

Characteristics of Reading Comprehension Tasks

The development of reading comprehension tasks was referenced to the *National Educational Standards (NES)* for English as a first foreign language (KMK, 2003, 2004), which list target reading comprehension competencies with reference to levels A2 and B1 of the *Common European Framework of Reference for Languages (CEF)* (Council of Europe, 2001), and to the CEF itself, which lists relevant proficiency descriptors for the levels A1 to C2.

A variety of methods is available for assessing reading comprehension across different assessment contexts (for an overview, see, e.g., Alderson, 2001; Alderson & Banerjee, 2002). Test formats are known to shape the assessed construct, because different item formats, in combinations with different types of questions, induce different reading comprehension processes (e.g., Cohen & Upton, 2006; Kobayashi, 2001; Rupp, Choi, & Ferne, 2006). However, it is not the choice of a particular response format *per se* that determines its appropriateness for assessing a given construct; rather, a careful selection of the text and construction of the items within this format determines the degree of validity of inferences about student proficiencies. Thus, each choice of a format represents a compromise between efficiency and construct representation in a particular application.

The operationalization of different types of reading comprehension in the tests developed by the IQB was summarized in *tables of specifications* for the tests, which essentially include information about (a) the types of reading comprehension targeted, (b) the text sources, discourse type, and topics of the input texts, (c) the concreteness, authenticity, format, and length of the texts, (d) the target language situation and original audience of the texts, and (e) the item types for each proficiency level in the CEF except for the highest (i.e., A1, A2, B1, B2, C1). This resulted in 10 different tables of specification where each formulation contained an explicit reference to both the English translation of the NES document and the English version of the CEF.

At the time of the publication of this report, the item writers had developed, between September 2005 and March 2007, a total of 393 reading comprehension items associated with 71 tasks or testlets that could be included in the field trial. Of the 71 tasks, 21 (30.0%) had items at different proficiency levels. Using a classification scheme where a task gets classified into the level that corresponds to the modal level of the item proficiency levels, the following distribution of proficiency levels across tasks existed in the item pool: A1 (5 tasks, 32 items), A2 (24 tasks, 124 items), B1 (26 tasks, 129 items), B2 (10 tasks, 72 items), C1 (6 tasks, 36 items).

Texts included prose, bullets, tables, graphs, and captions. Text length was modified according to the perceived proficiency level of the task and its associated items with overlap across the levels due to the well-established interaction between text length and other factors in accounting for variation in difficulty. Specifically, text length was distributed across proficiency levels as shown in table 8.1.

Table 8.1
Text Length for Tasks across Proficiency Levels

Level	Minimum	Maximum	Mean	Semi-IQR
A1	62	154	102	28
A2	65	288	163	57
B1	81	472	258	83
B2	272	553	387	60
C1	78	598	422	155

Note. IQR = Inter-quartile range (i.e., difference between the 75th and 25th percentile).

Texts at levels A1 to B1 contained *only or mostly frequent* vocabulary while texts at levels A2 to C1 contained *rather extended or extended* vocabulary. Texts at levels A1 and A2 contained *only or mainly simple* syntactic structures, texts at level B1 contained either *mainly simple* structures or a *limited range of complex* structures, and texts at levels B2 to C1 contained either a *limited or a wide range* of complex structures. Texts at level A1 contained *only concrete* content, texts at levels A2 and B1 contained *only or mostly concrete* content, and texts at levels B2 and C1 contained *mostly concrete or fairly abstract* content.

Texts could by classified as *descriptive, instructive, argumentative, narrative,* or *expository* and sometimes were multiply classified. Tasks at level A1 were mostly instructive or descriptive, tasks at level A2 were mostly descriptive, narrative, and expository, tasks at levels B1 and B2 had texts associated with all discourse structures, and tasks at level C1 had texts associated with all discourse structures but instructive ones; table 8.2 shows the sources that were used for texts and the topics that were covered with texts across all levels.

Item formats included *true-false-not given* (120 items), *multiple matching* (95 items), *short answer* (75 items), *multiple-choice* (50 items), *sequencing* (20 items), *table completion* (14 items), *sentence completion* (10 items), and *gap-filling* (9 items). Multiple-choice, multiple matching, and true-false-not given items were used across all proficiency levels while the other item types were used only at selected proficiency levels.

The majority of items at levels A1 and A2 are items that asked students to *scan* the text or do *search reading*, the majority of items at levels B1 to C1 asked students to determine the *main or overall idea* of a text when it is either explicitly or implicitly stated, and several items at these levels asked students to make *inferences* about the texts; table 8.3 lists the reading comprehension competencies that were assessed at each proficiency level.

Table 8.2
Text Sources, Text Types, and Topics for Reading Comprehension Tasks

Text Sources	Text Types	Topics
• Adverts	• Adverts	• Adventure and challenges
• Blurbs	• Articles	• Animals/animals and wildlife
• Books	• Blurbs	• Aspects of society
• Brochures	• Cartoons	• Celebrities
• CD/DVD covers	• CD/DVD covers	• Crime
• Comics	• Complex instructions	• Daily life
• Correspondences	• E-mails	• Education
• Encyclopedias	• Folk stories	• English speaking countries
• Internet	• Interviews	• Entertainment (e.g., sports, music)
• Leaflets	• Leaflets	• Environment
• Magazines	• Letters (personal)	• Festivals/customs
• Manuals	• Literature (extracts)	• Food and drink
• Menus	• Lyrics	• Free time
• Newspapers	• Manuals	• Global problems
• Posters	• Memos	• Health and body care
• Reference books	• Menus	• History
• Reviews	• Newspaper/ magazine articles	• House and home
• Signs	• Postcards	• Languages
• Youth magazines	• Programs	• Multicultural society
	• Recipes	• Personal identification
	• Reports	• Places
	• Reviews	• Relations with other people
	• Signs	• Science and technology
	• Simple instructions	• Service (e.g., museums, hospitals)
	• Short stories	• Shopping
	• SMS/text messages	• Travel
	• Text messages	• Weather
	• Timetables	• Work

Table 8.3
Reading Comprehension Competencies Assessed at Each Proficiency Level

Level	Reading Comprehension Competencies (*Learners can …*)
A1	1. understand the overall purpose 2. get an idea of the content of simple informational material and short simple descriptions, especially if there is visual support; follow short, simple written instructions 3. understand very short, simple texts, a single phrase at a time, picking up familiar names, words and basic phrases 4. deduce the meaning of words from the context, especially if there is visual support
A2	1. understand the overall idea (global: gist / skimming) 2. understand the main ideas and supporting details (detailed reading) 3. identify specific information (scanning / search reading) 4. deduce the probable meaning of unknown words from the context 5. make simple inferences (e.g., writer's intention / feelings / attitude towards something)
B1	1. understand the overall idea 2. understand the main ideas, implicit and explicit, line of argument, and supporting details 3. scan (longer) texts to locate information (also: search reading) 4. deduce the meaning of unknown words from the context 5. make inferences e.g., writer's intention / feelings / attitude towards something, recognize the author's main conclusions 6. collate information from different texts and / or different parts of a text (to solve a task)
B2	1. understand the overall idea / message 2. understand the main ideas of complex texts and supporting details 3. scan quickly long and / or complex texts, locating relevant details (also: search reading) 4. use contextual clues to achieve comprehension 5. make inferences e.g., author's stances / viewpoints and intentions and feelings towards something, recognize the author's main conclusions 6. obtain information, ideas and opinions from highly specialized sources within his / her field
C1	1. understand in detail lengthy, complex and demanding texts (both macro-propositional and propositional) 2. recognize implicit meaning 3. scan quickly through long and complex texts / locate relevant details 4. identify finer points of detail including moods, attitudes and implied and stated opinions 5. recognize stylistic variations

Characteristics of Listening Comprehension Tasks

The development of listening comprehension tasks was referenced to the *National Educational Standards (NES)* for English as a first foreign language (KMK, 2003, 2004), which list target reading comprehension competencies with reference to levels A2 and B1 of the *Common European Framework of Reference for Languages (CEF)* (Council of Europe, 2001), and to the CEF itself, which lists relevant proficiency descriptors for the levels A1 to C2.

A variety of methods are available for assessing listening comprehension across different assessment contexts, which are known to shape the assessed construct (for an overview, see, e.g., Alderson & Banerjee, 2002; Buck, 2001). As with the reading comprehension tasks above, it is not the choice of a particular response format *per se* that determines its appropriateness for assessing a given construct; rather, a careful selection of the text and construction of the items within this format determines the degree of validity of inferences about student proficiencies. Thus, each choice of a format represents a compromise between efficiency and construct representation in a particular application.

The operationalization of different types of listening comprehension in the tests developed by the IQB was summarized in *tables of specifications* for the tests, which essentially include information about (a) the types of listening comprehension targeted, (b) the input sources, discourse type, and topics of the input, (c) the concreteness, authenticity, format, and length of the input, (d) the target language situation and original audience of the input, and (e) the item types for each proficiency level in the CEF except for the highest (i.e., A1, A2, B1, B2, C1). This resulted in 10 different tables of specifications where each formulation contained an explicit reference to both the English translation of the NES document and the English version of the CEF.

At the time of the publication of this report, the item writers had developed, between September 2005 and March 2007, a total of 352 listening comprehension items associated with 65 tasks or testlets that could be included in the field trial. Out of the 65 tasks, 21 (32.3%) had items at different proficiency levels. Using a classification scheme where a task gets classified into the level that corresponds to the modal level of the item proficiency classifications, the following distribution of proficiency levels across tasks existed in the item pool: A1 (6 tasks, 19 items), A2 (21 tasks, 113 items), B1 (22 tasks, 137 items), B2 (11 tasks, 51 items), C1 (5 tasks, 32 items).

Of the 65 tasks, 38 (58.46%) used non-scripted authentic input, 17 (26.15%) used semi-scripted input, and 10 (15.38%) used scripted input with varying degrees of redundancy across all proficiency levels. Furthermore, 49 tasks (75.38%) across all proficiency levels were heard once by the students while the remaining 16 tasks (24.62%) were heard twice. Input could be classified as *descriptive, instructive, argumentative, narrative, expository*, or *phatic* and was sometimes multiply classified. However, tasks at level A1 were mostly instructive, tasks at level A2 were mostly instructive or narrative, tasks at levels B1 and B2 had input with all discourse structures, and tasks at level C1 were narrative or expository. The input was selected from a wide variety of sources and included a wide variety of text types across all proficiency levels; table 8.4 provides an overview.

Input length was modified according to the proficiency level of the task and its associated items with overlap across the levels due to the well-established interaction between input length and other factors in accounting for variation in task and item difficulty. Specifically, input length was distributed across the proficiency levels as follows: A1 – up to 2 minutes, A2 – up to 2.5 minutes, B1 – up to 3 minutes, B2 – up to 5 minutes, C1 – up to 7 minutes. The number of speakers similarly varied across proficiency levels (A1 and A2: 1-2 speakers, B1: 1-3 speakers, B2: 1-4 speakers, C1: 1-7 speakers) even though native and non-native, male and female, as well as young and old speakers were used across all levels. Speakers with a *British and American accent* were used for tasks across all proficiency levels, speakers with an *Irish accent* were used for task at levels A2 and B1, and one C1 task used a speaker with an *Australian accent*. 12 tasks (18.46%) across levels A1 to B2 also used non-native speakers.

Furthermore, the delivery was varied across the proficiency levels (A1: predominantly slowly (approx. 100-140 words per minute) and clearly articulated with pauses, A2: slowly and normal (approx. 150-190 words per minute), clearly articulated, B1: predominantly normal and clear articulation, B2: predominantly normal speed and articulation, C1: completely authentic in speed (approx. 160-200 words per minute) and articulation).

The content of the input was *only or mostly concrete* for tasks at levels A1 to B1, *mostly concrete or fairly abstract* for tasks at level B2, and *fairly or mainly abstract* for tasks at level C1. The vocabulary of the input was *only or mostly frequent* for tasks at levels A1 and A2, *mostly frequent* for tasks at levels B1 and B2, and *mainly extended or fairly abstract* for tasks at level C1. The syntactic structures of the input were *only or mainly simple* for tasks at levels A1 and A2, included *a limited range of complex structures* for some tasks at level B1, *a limited range of complex structures* for most tasks at levels B2 and C1, and even *a wide range of complex structures* for one C1 task. Out of the 65 input recordings, 54 (83.00%) did not contain any background noise. The recordings of a few tasks across all proficiency levels contained *supporting or distracting* noises and the recording for one task at level C1 contained *only distracting* noises.

Item formats included *multiple-choice* (124 items), *table completion* (108 items), *short answer* (89 items), *multiple matching* (22 items), and *note-taking* (9 items). At proficiency level A1 only multiple-choice items were used while note-taking items were used only at levels A2 and B1; otherwise, all item types were used across all proficiency levels. At each proficiency level there were items that asked the students to *identify specific information* and to *understand the main or overall ideas* of the input. Items at level A1 also measured whether students could *understand directions and instructions* while items at levels B1 to C1 also measured whether they could *make inferences*; table 8.5 provides an overview.

Table 8.4
Text Sources, Text Types, and Topics for Listening Comprehension Tasks

Text Sources	Text Types	Topics
• Internet	• Academic presentations	• Adventures and challenges
• Answering machines	• Ads	• Animals
• Audio Books	• Anecdotes	• Aspects of society
• Audio tours / guides	• Announcements	• Celebrities
• CD	• Commercials	• Crime
• DVD	• Conversations (phone-ins)	• Education / academia
• Live interviews	• Debates	• Entertainment
• Public announcements	• Dialogues	• Environment
• Radio	• Directions	• Everyday life (e.g., hobbies, friends)
• Private Recordings	• Discussions	• Festivals / customs
• Telephone	• Documentaries	• Food and drink
• TV	• Films	• Free time
	• Instructions	• Global problems
	• Interviews	• Health and body care
	• Jokes	• History
	• Lectures	• House and home
	• Limericks	• Multicultural society
	• Messages	• Places
	• Monologues	• Science and technology
	• Movies	• Services
	• News	• Shopping
	• News (radio, TV)	• Travelling
	• Plays	• Weather
	• Radio / Audio programs	• World of work
	• Reports	
	• Speeches	
	• Sports commentaries	
	• Stories	
	• Talk shows	
	• Talks	
	• Technical information	
	• Telephone conversations	
	• Weather forecast	

Table 8.5
Types of Listening Comprehension Competencies Assessed at Each Proficiency Level

Level	Listening Competencies Competencies (*Learners can …*)
A1	1. understand the overall idea / message / topic (very slow with long breaks) 2. get an idea of the topic of a simple conversation 3. understand instructions and follow short simple directions (with visual support) 4. recognize/identify specific information e.g., picking up familiar names, numbers, dates
A2	1. understand the overall idea / message / topic 2. understand the main ideas 3. identify specific information e.g., picking up familiar names, numbers, dates 4. make simple inferences regarding speaker's feelings / intentions, settings 5. can understand simple directions (e.g., relating to how to get from X to Y) / instructions 6. deduce the meaning of words from the context
B1	1. get a rough overview of the content (listen for gist; selective / global) 2. understand explicitly stated main ideas / supporting details; understand the main points (careful / local) 3. identify specific information (search listening; selective / local) 4. deduce the meaning of words from the context (careful / local) 5. make inferences about speaker's intention, attitude towards something, feelings (careful/global) 6. understand detailed directions / simple operating instructions for everyday equipment
B2	1. get an overview of the content (listen for gist; selective / global) 2. understand the main ideas / line of argument / speaker's viewpoints supporting details (in non-academic texts; careful / local) 3. identify specific information (search listening; selective / local) 4. deduce the meaning of words from the context 5. understand announcements and messages 6. understand technical instructions 7. make inferences about speaker's intention, attitude, mood, tone, feelings (careful / global)
C1	1. get an overview of the content of extended speech on abstract and complex topics which might be beyond the learner's field 2. understand main ideas / supporting details (both explicit and implicit) of extended speech on abstract and complex topics which might be beyond the learner's field 3. identify specific information including those from audibly distorted announcements 4. deduce the meaning of words from the context including idiomatic expressions and colloquialisms 5. make inferences e.g., about purpose, attitudes, relationships between speakers 6. understand complex technical information, specifications for familiar products and services 7. recognize different registers

Characteristics of Writing Tasks

The development of writing tasks was referenced to the *National Educational Standards (NES)* for English as a first foreign language (KMK, 2003, 2004), which list target reading comprehension competencies with reference to levels A2 and B1 of the *Common European Framework of Reference for Languages (CEF)* (Council of Europe, 2001), and to the CEF itself, which lists relevant proficiency descriptors for the levels A1 to C2.

A variety of methods are available for assessing writing (for an overview, see, e.g., Alderson & Banerjee, 2002; Weigle, 2002). As with the reading and listening constructs outlined above, the guiding documents for the development of writing test specifications at the IQB are the NES and the CEF.

At the time of the publication of this report, the item writers had developed, between September 2005 and March 2007, a total of 19 writing tasks that could be included in the field trial. Based on the NES, which list writing competencies with reference to the CEF levels A2 and B1, and based on relevant proficiency descriptors of the CEF for the levels A1 to C1, various types of writing were distinguished in tables of test specifications; table 8.7 provides an overview.

The expected length of texts varied by proficiency level with tasks associated with higher proficiency levels requiring longer texts (A1: 20-30 words, A2: 40-60 words, B1: 110-140 words, B2: 200-250 words, C1: 300-350 words). Consequently, the time allowed for the completion of each task varied by proficiency level as well, with tasks at higher proficiency levels being allotted more time (A1: 10 minutes, A2: 15 minutes, B1: 20 minutes, B2: 30 minutes, C1: 40 minutes). Similarly, the length of the prompt that students need to read in order to solve the task varies by proficiency level with tasks at a higher proficiency level having longer prompts, as shown in table 8.6.

Table 8.6
Length of Prompts for Tasks across Proficiency Levels

Level	Minimum	Maximum	Median	Semi-IQR
A1	27	80	51	22
A2	46	138	67	30
B1	46	117	89	22
B2	70	114	92	n.a.
C1	253	280	267	n.a.

Note. IQR = Inter-quartile range (i.e., difference between the 75th and 25th percentile). n.a. = not available as only two tasks were at these proficiency levels.

In terms of the discourse characteristics of the expected student responses, the tasks at level A1 and A2 ask for responses on *only concrete* content, the tasks at level B1 ask for *mostly concrete* content, and the tasks at levels B2 and C1 ask for *mostly concrete or fairly abstract* content. The expected text could be classified as *descriptive, instructive, argumentative, narrative, expository,* or *phatic* and was sometimes multiply classified. However, tasks at level A1 were only descriptive, tasks at level A2 were descriptive, phatic, or instructive, tasks at levels B1 had all discourse structures except narrative texts, texts at level B2 were instructive, argumentative, and descriptive, and texts at level C1 had all discourse structures except instructive texts. The tasks are written for a wide range of writing purposes that are listed in table 8.7 for tasks at all proficiency levels.

Table 8.7
Writing Competencies Assessed at Each Proficiency Level

Level	Writing Competencies (*Learners can ...*)
A1	1. write groups of words / simple isolated phrases and sentences 2. fill in simple forms 3. ask for or pass on personal details in written form 4. write a short simple postcard 5. write simple phrases and sentences about themselves and imaginary people.
A2	1. write groups of words / phrases / sentences 2. write short and simple (formulaic) notes, messages and posters 3. write very simple personal letters and emails 4. write short simple texts
B1	1. write straightforward detailed texts 2. write notes and messages 3. write personal letters, simple formal letters and emails 4. write short reports / articles
B2	1. write clear, detailed connected texts 2. write a description, a review, an essay or report 3. express news and views and relate to those of others 4. write formal and informal letters 5. write an argumentative text, giving reasons in support of or against a particular point of view and explaining the advantages and disadvantages 6. evaluate different ideas or solutions to a problem
C1	1. write clear, well-structured texts (reports, articles, essays, descriptions, expositions, comments) 2. write clear, detailed, well-structured and developed descriptions and imaginative texts 3. write formal and informal letters

More specifically, they can be distinguished by the speech acts they elicit either in isolation or in conjunction; table 8.8 provides an overview of the range of speech acts for tasks across all proficiency levels.

Table 8.8
Speech Acts for Writing Tasks

Speech Acts
- to appeal
- to attract interest
- to comment
- to describe
- to evaluate
- to excuse
- to explain
- to express experiences / feelings
- to express opinions / viewpoints / preferences
- to give advice / ask for advice
- to give arguments
- to give directions
- to inform / to ask for information
- to instruct
- to invite
- to make arrangements
- to persuade / convince
- to provide support
- to state advantages / disadvantages
- to summarize
- to tell a story
- to thank / apologize
- to give directions

References

Alderson, J. C. (1990). Bands and scores. In J. C. Alderson, & B. North (Eds.), *Language Testing in the 1990s: The communicative legacy* (pp. 71-86). London: Macmillan.

Alderson, J. C. (2000). *Assessing reading*. Cambridge: Cambridge University Press.

Alderson, J. C., & Banerjee, J. (2002). State-of-the-art review: Language testing and assessment (Part II). *Language Teaching, 35,* 79-113.

Alderson, J. C., & Huhta, A. (2005). The development of a suite of computer-based diagnostic tests based on the Common European Framework. *Language Testing, 22,* 301-320.

Alderson, J. C., Figueras, N., Kuijper, H., Nold, G., Takala, S., & Tardieu, C. (2006). Analysing tests of reading and listening in relation to the common European framework of reference: The experience of the Dutch CEFR construct project. *Language Assessment Quarterly, 3,* 3-30.

Bachman, L. F. (1990). *Fundamental considerations in language testing*. Oxford/NY: Oxford University Press.

Bachman, L. F. (2005). Building and supporting a case for test use. *Language Assessment Quarterly, 2*(1), 1-34.

Bachman, L. F., & Palmer, A. S. (1996). *Language testing in practice*. Oxford: Oxford University Press.

Bae, J., & Bachman, L. (1998). A latent variable approach to listening and reading: Testing factorial invariance across two groups of children in the Korean/English two-way immersion program. *Language Testing, 15,* 380-414.

Baumert, J., Bos, W., & Lehmann, R. (Eds.). (2000). *TIMSS III. Dritte Internationale Mathematik- und Naturwissenschaftsstudie – Mathematische und naturwissenschaftliche Grundbildung am Ende der Pflichtschulzeit* [TIMSS III. Third International Mathe and Science Study – Mathematical and scientific literacy at the end of schooling]. Opladen: Leske & Budrich.

Baumert, J., Klieme, E., Neubrand, M., Prenzel, M., Schiefele, U., Schneider, W., Stanat, P., Tillmann, K. J., & Weiß, M. (Eds.). (2001). *PISA 2000 – Basiskompetenzen von Schülerinnen und Schülern im internationalen Vergleich [PISA 2000 – An international comparison of basic competencies]*. Opladen: Leske & Budrich.

Beck, B., & Klieme, E. (Eds.). (2007). *Sprachliche Kompetenzen – Konzepte und Messungen. DESI Ergebnisse Band 1* [Linguistic competences – constructs and their measurement. Results from DESI Volume 1]. Weinheim: Beltz.

Bejar, I., Douglas, D., Jamieson, J., Nissan, S., & Turner, J. (2000). *TOEFL 2000 listening framework: A working paper* (Research report No. RR-00-7). Princeton, NJ: Educational Testing Service.

Bereiter, C. (1980). Development in writing. In L. W. Gregg, & E. R. Steinberg (Eds.), *Cognitive processes in writing* (pp. 73-93). Hillsdale, NJ: Erlbaum.

Bereiter, C., & Scardamalia, M. (1987). *The psychology of written composition*. Hillsdale, NJ: Erlbaum.

Bock, R. D., Brennan, R. L., & Muraki, E. (2000). The information in multiple ratings. *Applied Psychological Measurement, 26,* 264-375.

Börner, W. (1989). Didaktik schriftlicher Textproduktion in der Fremdsprache [The didactics of written composition in a foreign language]. In G. Antons, & H. P. Krings (Eds.), *Textproduktion. Ein interdisziplinärer Forschungsüberblick [Text production: An interdisciplinary research review]* (pp. 348-376). Tübingen: Niemeyer.

Bos, W., Lankes, E. M., Prenzel, M., Schwippert, K., Walther, G., & Valtin, R. (Eds.). (2003). *Erste Ergebnisse aus IGLU. Schülerleistungen am Ende der vierten Jahr-

gangsstufe im Vergleich [First results from PIRLS/IGLU. Student achievement at the end of 4th grade]. Münster: Waxmann.

Brennan, R. L. (2001). *Generalizability theory*. New York: Springer.

Brindley, G. (1998). Describing language development? Rating scales and SLA. In L. F. Bachman, & A. D. Cohen (Eds.), *Interfaces between second language acquisition and language testing research* (pp. 112-140). Cambridge: Cambridge University Press.

Brindley, G., & Slatyer, H. (2002). Exploring task difficulty in ESL listening assessment. *Language Testing, 19*(4), 369-394.

Brown, D. (1994). *Principles of language learning and teaching*. Englewood Cliffs: Prentice Hall.

Brown, G. (1995). Dimensions of difficulty in listening comprehension. In D. J. Mendelsohn, & J. Rubin (Eds.), *A guide for the teaching of second language listening* (pp. 59-73). Carlsbad, CA: Dominie Press.

Buck, G. (1991). The testing of listening comprehension: An introspective study. *Language Testing, 8*(1), 67-91.

Buck, G. (2001). *Assessing listening*. Cambridge: Cambridge University Press.

Buck, G., & Tatsuoka, K. (1998). Application of the rule-space procedure to language testing: Examining attributes of a free response listening test. *Language Testing, 15*(2), 119-157.

Buck, G., Tatsuoka, K., & Kostin, I. (1997). The subskills of reading: Rule-space analysis of a multiple-choice test of second language reading comprehension. *Language Learning, 47,* 423-466.

Butler, F. A., Eignor, D., Jones, S., McNamara, T., & Suomi, B. K. (2000). *TOEFL 2000 speaking framework: A working paper* (Research Report No. RM-00-6). Princeton, NJ: Educational Testing Service.

Byram, M. (1997). *Teaching and assessing intercultural communicative competence*. Clevedon: Multilingual Matters.

Camp, R. (1996). New views on measurement and new models for writing assessment. In E. White, W. Lutz, & S. Kamusikiri (Eds.), *Assessment of writing: Politics, policies, practices* (pp. 135-147). NY: MLAA.

Canale, M. (1983). From communicative competence to communicative language pedagogy. In J. Richards & R. W. Schmidt (Eds.), *Language and communication* (pp. 2-28). London: Longman.

Canale, M., & Swain, M. (1980). Theoretical bases of communicative approaches to second language teaching and testing. *Applied Linguistics, 1,* 1-47.

Carver, R. P. (1997). Reading for one second, one minute, or one year from the perspective of rauding theory. *Scientific Studies of Reading, 1,* 3-43.

Chapelle, C. (2006). DIALANG: A diagnostic language test in 14 European languages [Test review]. *Language Testing, 23,* 544-550.

Chapelle, C., Grabe, W., & Berns, M. (1997). *Communicative language proficiency: Definitions and implications for TOEFL 2000* (ETS Research Report RM-97-3). Princeton, NJ: Educational Testing Service.

Chiappe, P., Hasher, L., & Siegel, L. S. (2000). Working memory, inhibitory control, and reading disability. *Memory & Cognition, 28,* 8-17.

Chiu, C. W. T., & Wolfe, E. W. (2002). A method for analyzing sparse data matrices in the generalizability theory framework. *Applied Psychological Measurement, 26,* 321-338.

Cizek, G. J., Bunch, M. B., & Koons, H. (2004). Setting performance standards: Contemporary methods. *Educational Measurement: Issues and Practice, 23,* 31-50. Available online at www.ncme.org

Cohen, A. D., & Upton, T. A. (2006). *Strategies in responding to New TOEFL reading tasks* (TOEFL Monograph Report MS-33). Princeton, NJ: Educational Testing Service.

Congdon, P. J., & McQueen, J. (2000). The stability of rater severity in large-scale assessment programs. *Journal of Educational Measurement, 37,* 163-178.

Coniam, D. (1998). Interactive evaluation of listening comprehension: How the context may help. *Computer Assisted Language Learning, 11,* 35-53.

Cortina, K. S., Baumert, J., Leschinsky, A., Mayer, K. U., & Trommer, L. (Eds.). (2003). *Das Bildungswesen in der Bundesrepublik Deutschland: Strukturen und Entwicklungen im Überblick* [The educational system in Germany: A review of ist structure and developments]. Hamburg: Rohwolt.

Council of Europe (2001). *Common European reference framework for languages.* Available online at www.coe.int/T/DG4/Portfolio/?L=E&M=/documents_intro/common_framework.html

Council of Europe (2003). *Relating language examinations to the Common European Framework of Reference for Languages: Learning, Teaching, Assessment (CEF). Manual, preliminary pilot version.* Strasbourg. Available online at http://www.coe.int/T/DG4/Portfolio/?L=E&M=/documents_intro/Manual.html

Cumming, A. (1990). Expertise in evaluating second language compositions. *Language Testing, 7,* 31-51.

Cumming, A. (1998). Theoretical perspectives on writing. In W. Grabe (Ed.), *Foundations of second language teaching. Annual Review of Applied Linguistics, 18* (pp. 61-78). Cambridge: University Press.

Cumming, A., Kantor, R., & Powers, D. (2001). *Scoring TOEFL essays and TOEFL 2000 prototype writing tasks: An investigation into raters' decision-making, and development of a preliminary analytic framework* (TOEFL Monograph Series). Princeton, NJ: Educational Testing Service.

Cumming, A., Kantor, R., Powers, D., Santos, T., & Taylor, C. (2000). *TOEFL 2000 writing framework: A working paper* (Research report No. RR-00-5). Princeton, NJ: Educational Testing Service.

Deane, P. (2006). Strategies for evidence identification through linguistic assessment of textual responses. In D. M. Williamson, R. J. Mislevy, & I. I. Bejar (Eds.), *Automated scoring of complex tasks in computer based testing* (pp. 313-371). Mahwah, NJ: Erlbaum.

Der Spiegel (2007). *Widerstand gegen das Pflichtfach Französisch am Gymnasium am Oberrhein* (Ausgabe 18-2007) [Resistance against French as a mandatory subject in grammar school at the upper Rhine valley]. Hamburg: Verlag Der Spiegel.

Doughty, C., & Long, M. H. (Eds.). (2005). *Handbook of second language acquisition.* London: Blackwell.

Droop, M. V., & Verhoeven, L. (1998). Background knowledge, linguistic complexity, and second-language reading comprehension. *Journal of Literacy Research, 30,* 253-271.

Eckes, T. (2005). Examining rater effects in TestDaF writing and speaking performance assessments: A many-facet Rasch analysis. *Language Assessment Quarterly, 2,* 197-221.

Eckes, T., & Grotjahn, R. (2006). A closer look at the construct validity of C-tests. *Language Testing, 23,* 290-325.

Educational Testing Service (2000). *Test of English as a foreign language (TOEFL).* Princeton, NJ: Educational Testing Service.

Ellis, R., & Widdowson, H. G. (1997). *Second language acquisition: An introduction.* Oxford: Oxford University Press.

Enright, M. K., Grabe, W., Koda, K., Mosenthal, P., Mulcahy-Ernt, P., & Schedl, M. (2000). *TOEFL 2000 Reading Framework: A working paper* (TOEFL Monograph Series Nr. MS-17). Princeton, NJ: Educational Testing Service.

Ericsson, K. A., & Simon, H. A. (1993). *Protocol analysis: Verbal reports as data (revised edition)*. Cambridge, MA: MIT Press.

Eurobarometer (2006). *Europeans and their languages* (Special Eurobarometer 243). Available online at http://ec.europa.eu/public_opinion/archives/ebs/ebs_243_en.pdf

Fachverband Deutscher Sprachreise Veranstalter (FDSV) (2006). *Marktanalyse zu Sprachreisen in 2005* [Market survey of language-related travel]. Available online at http://www.fdsv.de/fdsv/site/fdsv_fsmain.php

Finkenstaedt, T., & Schröder, K. (1992). *Sprachen im Europa von morgen* [The languages of Europe in the future]. Berlin: Langenscheidt.

Fitzgerald, J. (1995). English-as-a-second-language learners' cognitive reading processes: A review of research in the United States. *Review of Educational Research, 65,* 145-190.

Freedle, R., & Kostin, I. (1991). *The prediction of SAT reading comprehension item difficulty for expository prose passages* (Research Report RR 91-29). Princeton, NJ: Educational Testing Service.

Freedle, R., & Kostin, I. (1992). *The prediction of GRE reading comprehension item difficulty for expository prose passages for each of three item types: Main Ideas, inferences, and explicit statements* (Research Report RR 91-59). Princeton, NJ: Educational Testing Service.

Freedle, R., & Kostin, I. (1993). The prediction of TOEFL reading item difficulty: Implications for construct validity. *Language Testing, 10,* 133-170.

Freedle, R., & Kostin, I. (1999). Does the text matter in a multiple-choice test of listening comprehension? The case for the construct validity of TOEFL's minitalks. *Language Testing, 16,* 2-32.

Fulcher, G. (1995). Variable competence in second language acquisition: a problem for research methodology? In *System, 23*(1), 25-33.

Gass, S. M., & Selinker, L. (2001). *Second language acquisition: An introductory course* (2nd ed.). Mahwah, NJ: Erlbaum.

Gernsbacher, M. A. (1990). *Language comprehension as structure building*. Hillsdale, NJ: Erlbaum.

Gernsbacher, M. A. (1997). Two decades of structure building. *Discourse Processes, 23,* 265-304.

Gilmore, A. (2007) Authentic materials and authenticity in foreign language learning. *Language Teacher, 40,* 97-118.

Ginther, A. (2001). *Effects of the presence and absence of visuals on performance on TOEFL® CBT listening-comprehension stimuli* (TOEFL Research Report 66). Princeton, NJ: Educational Testing Service.

Goh, C. C. (2000). A cognitive perspective on language learners' listening comprehension problems. *System, 28*(1), 55-75.

Gorin, J. S. (2002). *Cognitive and psychometric modeling of text-based reading comprehension GRE-V test items*. Unpublished doctoral dissertation, University of Kansas.

Gorin, J. S. (in press). Manipulating processing difficulty of reading comprehension questions: Another step towards item generation. *Applied Psychological Measurement*.

Grabe, W., & Kaplan, R. B. (1996). *Theory & practice of writing: An applied linguistic perspective*. Harlow, England: Pearson Education.

Grotjahn, R. (2000). Kognitive Determinanten der Schwierigkeit von fremdsprachlichen Lese- und Hörverstehensaufgaben. Zur Prognose der Aufgabenschwierigkeit in Sprachtests [Predicting the difficulty in reading and listening comprehension tasks

via cognitive factors]. In C. Riemer (Ed.), *Kognitive Aspekte des Lehrens und Lernens von Fremdsprachen. Festschrift für Willis J. Edmonson zum 60. Geburtstag* (pp. 338-353). Tübingen: Gunter Narr.
Gruba, P. (1997). Exploring digital video material. In R. Debski, J. Gassin, & M. Smith (Eds.), *Language Learning Through Social Computing* (pp. 109-140). Parkville Vic: Applied Linguistics Association of Australia.
Hale, G. A., & Courtney, R. (1994). The effects of note-taking on listening comprehension in the Test of English as a Foreign Language. *Language Testing, 11*, 29-47.
Hamp-Lyons, L. (1990). Second language writing: Assessment issues. In B. Kroll (Ed.), *Second Language Writing: Research insights for the classroom* (pp. 69-87). Cambridge: Cambridge University Press.
Hamp-Lyons, L. (1996). The challenges of second-language writing assessment. In E. White, W. Lutz, & S. Kamusikiri (Eds), *Assessment of writing: Politics, Policies, Practices* (pp. 226-240). New York: MLAA.
Harsch, C. (2007). *Der gemeinsame europäische Referenzrahmen für Sprachen. Leistung und Grenzen* [The Common European Framework of Reference: Strengths and Limitations]. Saarbrücken: VDM Verlag Dr. Müller.
Harsch, C., Neumann, A., Lehmann, H. R., & Schröder, K. (2007). Schreibfähigkeit [Writing ability]. In B. Beck & E. Klieme (Eds.), *Sprachliche Kompetenzen: Konzepte und Messung* [Linguistic Competencies: Concepts and Assessment]. *DESI-Studie* (pp. 42-62). Weinheim: Beltz.
Hartig, J., & Frey, A. (2005, September). *Ein Vergleich verschiedener erklärender Item-response-Modelle in der modellbasierten Kompetenzskalierung* [A comparison of different explanatory item repsponse theory models in model-based proficiency scaling]. Paper presented at the 7. Fachtagung der Fachgruppe Methoden und Evaluation der Deutschen Gesellschaft für Psychologie, Münster, Germany.
Hawkey, R., & Barker, F. (2004). Developing a common scale for the assessment of writing. *Assessing Writing, 9*, 122-159.
Hayes, J. R. (1996). A new framework for understanding cognition and affect in writing. In C. M. Levy, & S. Ransdell (Eds.), *The science of writing. Theories, methods, individual differences and applications* (pp. 1-27). Hillsdale, NJ: Lawrence Erlbaum.
Hayes, J. R., & Flower, S. L. (1980). Identifying the organization of writing processes. In L. W. Gregg, & E. R. Steinberg (Eds.), *Cognitive processes in writing* (pp. 31-50). Hillsdale, NJ: Erlbaum.
Henning, G. (1990). *A study of the effects of variation of short-term memory load, reading response length, and processing hierarchy on TOEFL listening comprehension item performance* (TOEFL Research Report RR-90-18). Princeton, NJ: Educational Testing Service.
Hoien, T., Lundberg, I., Stanovich, K. E., & Bjaalid, I-K. (1995). Components of phonological awareness. *Reading and Writing, 7*, 171-188.
Hosenfeld, I., Ophoff, J. G., & Bittins, P. (2006). Vergleichsarbeiten und Schulentwicklung [Large-scale assessment and school development]. *Schulmanagement Handbuch,* 118.
Hyland, K. (2002). *Teaching and researching writing*. London: Pearson Education.
Hyland, K. (2003). *Second language writing*. Cambridge: Cambridge University Press.
Jamieson, J., Jones, S., Kirsch, I., Mosenthal, P., & Taylor, C. (2000). *TOEFL 2000 framework: A working paper* (Research Report RM-00-3). Princeton, NJ: Educational Testing Service.
Jensen, C., & Hansen, C. (1995). The effect of prior knowledge on EAP listening test performance. *Language Testing, 12*, 99-119.
Jensen, C., Hansen, C., Green, S., & Akey, T. (1997). An investigation of item difficulty incorporating the structure of listening tests: A hierarchical linerar modeling

analysis. In A. Huhta, V. Kohonen, L. Kurki-Suonio, & S. Luoma (Eds.), *Current developments and alternatives in language assessment* (pp. 151-164). Jyväskylä: University of Jyväskylä.

Kaga, M. (1991). Dictation as a measure of Japanese proficiency. *Language Testing, 8,* 112-24.

Kintsch, W. (1998). *Comprehension: A paradigm for cognition.* New York: Cambridge University Press.

Kirsch, I. S., & Mosenthal, P. B. (1990). Exploring document literacy: Variables underlying the performance of young adults. *Reading Research Quarterly, 25,* 5-30.

Kirsch, I. S., & Mosenthal, P. B. (1995). Interpreting the IEA reading literacy scales. In M. Binkley, K. Rust, & M. Winglee (Eds.), *Methodological issues in comparative educational studies: The case of the IEA reading literacy study* (pp. 135-192). Washington, DC: Department of Education, National Center for Education Statistics.

Klieme, E., Avenarius, H., Blum, W., Döbrich, P., Gruber, H., Prenzel, M., Reiss, K., Riquarts, K., Rost, J., Tenorth, H.-E., & Vollmer, H. J. (2003). *Zur Entwicklung nationaler Bildungsstandards: Eine Expertise* [The development of national educational standards]. Berlin: Bundesministerium für Bildung und Forschung.

KMK (2003). *Bildungsstandards für die erste Fremdsprache (Englisch/Französisch) für den Mittleren Abschluss* [National educational standards for the first foreign language (English/French) for the Mittlerer Schulabschluss]. Darmstadt: Luchterhand.

KMK (2004). *Bildungsstandards für die erste Fremdsprache (Englisch/Französisch) für den Hauptschulabschluss* [National educational standards for the first foreign language (English/French) for the Hauptschulabschluss]. Darmstadt: Luchterhand.

KMK (2006). *Gesamtstrategie der Kultusministerkonferenz zum Bildungsmonitoring* [Strategic plan of the educational council for educational systems-monitoring in Germany]. Neuwied: Wolters-Kluwe.

Kobayashi, M. (2002). Method effects on reading comprehension test performance: Text organization and response format. *Language Testing, 19,* 193-220.

Krapels, A. R. (1990). An overview of second language writing process research. In B. Kroll (Ed.), *Second language writing: Research insights for the classroom* (pp. 37-56). Cambridge: Cambridge University Press.

Kroll, B. (1998). Assessing writing abilities. *Annual Review of Applied Linguistics, 18,* 219-240.

Lehmann, R. H. (1990). Aufsatzbeurteilung – Forschungsstand und empirische Daten [Scoring essays – Current state-of-the-art and empirical results]. In K. Ingenkamp, & R. Jäger (Eds.), *Tests und Trends 8* (pp. 64-94). Weinheim: Beltz.

Lehmann, R. H. (1994). Research on national and international writing assessments: Contributions from the Hamburg Study of Achievement in Written Composition. In R. Ansorge (Ed.), *Schlaglichter der Forschung. Zum 75. Jahrestag der Gründung der Universität Hamburg 1994. Hamburger Beiträge zur Wissenschaftsgeschichte (Band 15)* (pp. 173-184). Hamburg: Reimer.

Leighton, J. P. (2004). Avoiding misconception, misuse, and missed opportunities: The collection of verbal reports in educational achievement testing. *Educational Measurement: Issues & Practice, 23*(4), 6-15.

Lesaux, N., Rupp, A. A., & Siegel, L. S. (in press). Growth in reading skills of children from diverse linguistic backgrounds: Findings from a 5-year longitudinal study. *Journal of Educational Psychology.*

Little, D. (2006). The Common European Framework of Reference for Languages: Content, purpose, origin, reception, and impact. *Language Teaching, 39,* 167-190.

Long, D. R. (1990). What you don't know can't help you. An exploratory study of background knowledge and second language listening comprehension. *Studies in Second Language Learning, REM Check 12,* 65-80.

Lumley, T. (2002). Assessment criteria in a large-scale writing test: What do they really mean to the raters? *Language Testing, 19,* 246-276.

Massaro, D. (1994). Psychological aspects of speech perception: Implications for research and theory. In M. A. Gernsbacher (Ed.), *Handbook of Psycholinguistics* (pp. 219-263). San Diego: Academic Press.

McClelland, J., & Elman, J. (1986). The TRACE model of speech perception. *Cognitive Psychology, 18,* 1-86.

McDougall, S., Hulme, C., Ellis, A., & Monk, A. (1994). Learning to read: The role of short-term memory and phonological processing skills. *Journal of Experimental Child Psychology, 58,* 112-133.

McKay, P. (2005). Research into the assessment of school-age language learners. Annual *Review of Applied Linguistics, 25,* 243-263.

McNamara, D. S., & Kintsch, W. (1996). Learning from texts: Effects of prior knowledge and text coherence. *Discourse Processes, 22,* 247-288.

Metsala, J. L., Stanovich, K. E., & Brown, G. D. A. (1998). Regularity effects and the phonological deficit model of reading disabilities: A meta-analytic review. *Journal of Educational Psychology, 90,* 273-292.

Milanovic, M., Saville, N., & Shuhong, S. (1996). A study of the decision-making behaviour of composition markers. In M. Milanovic, & N. Saville (Eds.), *Language testing 3 – Performance, testing, cognition and assessment* (pp. 92-114). Cambridge: Cambridge University Press.

Möller, J., & Schiefele, U. (2004). Motivationale Grundlagen der Lesekompetenz [The motivational basis of reading comprehension]. In U. Schiefele, C. Artelt, W. Schneider, & P. Stanat (Eds.), Entwicklung, Bedingungen und Förderungen der Lesekompetenz: Vertiefende Analysen der PISA-2000-Daten [Development, conditions and facilitation of Reading Competencies. In-depth analyses of data from PISA 2000] (pp. 101-124). Wiesbaden: Verlag für Sozialwissenschaften.

Mosenthal, P. B. (1996). Understanding the strategies of document literacy and their conditions of use. *Journal of Educational Psychology, 88,* 314-332.

Neisser, U. (1994). Multiple systems: A new approach to cognitive theory. *The European Journal of Cognitive Psychology, 6,* 225-242.

Nissan, S., deVincenzi, F., & Tang, K. L. (1996). *An analysis of factors affecting the difficulty of dialogue items in TOEFL listening comprehension* (TOEFL Research Report No. 51). Princeton, NJ: Educational Testing Service.

Neumann, A. (2005). *Dimensionen der Schreibfähigkeit. Differenzierte Analysen der Texte aus DESI und LAU11/ULME1* [Dimensions of writing ability: A differentiated analysis of the texts in DESI and LAU11/UMLE1]. Unpublished doctoral dissertation, University of Hamburg, Germany.

Nold, G., & Willenberg, H. (2007). Lesefähigkeit [Reading comprehension]. In B. Beck, & E. Klieme (Eds.), *Sprachliche Kompetenzen: Konzepte und Messung. DESI-Studie* (pp. 23-41). Weinheim: Beltz.

Nold, G., & Rossa, H. (2007). Hörverstehen [Listening comprehension]. In B. Beck, & E. Klieme (Eds.), *Sprachliche Kompetenzen. Konzepte und Messung. DESI-Studie* (pp. 178-196). Weinheim: Beltz.

North, B. (1996). *The development of a common framework scale of language proficiency.* New York: Lang.

North, B. (2000). Linking language assessments: an example in a low stakes context. *System 28*(4), 555-577.

North, B. (2002). A CEF-based self assessment tool for university entrance. In J. C. Alderson (Ed.), *Common European Framework of Reference for Languages: learning, teaching and assessment. Case studies* (pp. 146-166). Strasbourg: Council of Europe.

North, B., & Schneider, G. (1998). Scaling descriptors for language proficiency scales. *Language Testing, 15*, 217-263.

Papageorgiou, S. (2007). *Relating the Trinity College London GESE and ISE exams to the Common European Framework of Reference: Piloting of the Council of Europe Draft Manual* (Unpublished final project report). London: Trinity College.

Pennington, M. C. (2003). The impact of the computer in second language writing. In B. Kroll (Ed.), *Exploring the dynamics of second language writing* (pp. 287-310). Cambridge: Cambridge University Press.

Perfetti, C. A. (1997). Sentences, individual differences, and multiple texts: Three issues in text comprehension. *Discourse Processes, 23*, 337-355.

Polio, C. (2003). Research on second language writing. An overview of what we investigate and how. In B. Kroll (Ed.), *Exploring the dynamics of second language writing* (pp. 287-310). Cambridge: Cambridge University Press.

Prenzel, M., Baumert, J., Blum, W., Lehmann, R., Leutner, D., Neubrand, M., Pekrun, R., Rolff, H.-G., Rost, J., & Schiefele, U. (Eds.). (2004). *PISA 2003. Der Bildungsstand der Jugendlichen in Deutschland – Ergebnisse des zweiten internationalen Vergleichs* [PISA 2003: Achievement profiles of adolescents in Germany – Results from the second international comparison]. Münster: Waxmann.

RAND Reading Study Group. (2002). *Reading for understanding: Toward an R&D program in reading comprehension*. Washington, DC: RAND Education.

Rost, D. H. (1991). Reading comprehension: Skill or skills? *Journal of Research in Reading, 12*, 85-113.

Rost, D. H. (1993). Assessing different components of reading comprehension: Fact or fiction? *Language Testing, 10*, 79-92.

Rost, J. (2004). Psychometrische Modelle zur Überprüfung von Bildungsstandards anhand von Kompetenzmodellen [Psychometric models for the empirical investigation of national educational standards via theoretical models of competence]. *Zeitschrift für Pädagogik, 50*, 662-679.

Rost, M. (1990). *Listening in language learning*. London: Longman.

Rost, M. (2002). *Teaching and researching listening*. Harlow: Pearson Education.

Rumelhart, D. E. (1994). Toward an interactive model of reading. In R. B. Ruddell, M. Rapp, & H. Singer (Eds.), *Theoretical models and processes of reading (4th Ed.)* (pp. 864-894). Newark, DE: International Reading Association.

Rupp, A. A., Choi, H., & Ferne, T. (2006). How assessing reading comprehension with multiple-choice questions shapes the construct: A cognitive processing perspective. *Language Testing, 23*, 1-34.

Rupp, A., Garcia, P., & Jamieson, J. (2001). Combining multiple regression and CART to understand difficulty in second language reading and listening comprehension test items. *International Journal of Testing, 1*, 185-216.

Rupp, A. A., & Vock, M. (2007). National educational standards in Germany: Methodological challenges for developing and calibrating standards-based tests. In D. Waddington, P. Nentwig, & S. Schanze (Eds.), *Making it comparable. Standards in science education* (pp. 173-198). Münster: Waxmann.

Schachter, J. (1990). *Communicative competence revisited*. The development of second language proficiency. Cambridge: CUP.

Schaffner, E., Schiefele, U., & Schneider, W. (2004). Ein erweitertes Verständnis der Lesekompetenz: Die Ergebnisse des nationalen Ergänzungstests [An extended construct definition of reading ability: The results of the national extension studies].

In U. Schiefele, C. Artelt, W. Schneider, & P. Stanat (Eds.), *Struktur, Entwicklung und Förderung von Lesekompetenz: Vertiefende Analysen im Rahmen von PISA 2000* [Development, conditions and facilitation of reading competencies. In-depth analyses of data from PISA 2000] (pp. 197-242). Wiesbaden: VS Verlag für Sozialwissenschaften, 2004.

Schecker, H., & Parchmann, I. (2007). Standards and competence models: The German situation. In D. Waddington, P. Nentwig, & S. Schanze (Eds.), *Making it comparable. Standards in science education* (pp. 147-164). Münster: Waxmann.

Schmidt, R. (Ed.). (1995). Attention and awareness in foreign language learning (Technical Report Series, Vol. 9). Honolulu: University of Hawai'i Press.

Schnotz, W., & Dutke, S. (2004). Kognitionspsychologische Grundlagen der Lesekompetenz: Mehrebenenverarbeitung anhand multipler Informationsquellen [Cognitive foundations of reading comprehension: Multi-level processing using multiple sources of information]. In U. Schiefele, C. Artelt, W. Schneider, & P. Stanat (Eds.), *Struktur, Entwicklung und Förderung von Lesekompetenz. Vertiefende Analysen im Rahmen von PISA 2000* [Development, conditions and facilitation of Reading Competencies. In-depth analyses of data from PISA 2000] (pp. 61-99). Wiesbaden: VS Verlag für Sozialwissenschaften.

Sherman, J. (1997). The effect of question preview in listening comprehension tests. *Language Testing, 14,* 185-213.

Shermis, M. D., & Burstein, J. (2003). *Automated essay scoring: A cross-disciplinary perspective.* Hillsdale, NJ: Lawrence Erlbaum.

Shohamy, E. (1996). Competence and performance in language testing. In G. Brown, K. Malmkjoer, & J. Williams (Eds.), *Performance and competence in second language acquisition* (pp. 136-151). Cambridge: Cambridge University Press.

Shohamy, E., & Inbar, O. (1991). Construct validation of listening comprehension tests: The effect of text and question type. *Language Testing, 8,* 23-40.

Shohamy, E., Gordon, C., & Kraemer, R. (1992). The effect of raters' background and training on the reliability of direct writing tests. *Modern Language Journal, 76,* 27-33.

Siegel, L. S. (1993). The development of reading. In H. W. Reese (Ed.), *Advances in child development and behavior* (pp. 63-97). San Diego: Academic Press.

Stansfield, C. W., Scott, M. L., & Kenyon, D. M. (1990). *Listening summary translation exam (LSTE) – Spanish* (Final project report. ERIC Document Reproduction Service, ED 323 786). Washington, DC: Center for Applied Linguistics.

Stansfield, C. W., Wu, W. M., & Liu, C. C. (1997). *Listening Summary Translation Exam (LSTE) in Taiwanese, aka Minnan* (Final project report. ERIC Document Reproduction Service, ED 413 788). N. Bethesda, MD: Second Language Testing, Inc.

Stansfield, C. W., Wu, W. M., & van der Heide, M. (2000). A job-relevant listening summary translation exam in Minnan. In A. J. Kunnan (Ed.), *Fairness and validation in language assessment* (Studies in Language Testing Series, Vol. 9, pp. 177-200). Cambridge: Cambridge University Press.

Tankó, G. (2005). *Into Europe: Prepare for modern English exams. The writing handbook.* Budapest: Teleki László Foundation.

Tannenbaum, R. J., & Wylie, E. C. (2005). *Mapping English language proficiency test scores onto the Common European Framework* (Research Report No. RR-80). Princeton, NJ: Educational Testing Service.

Trinity College London. (2005a). *Graded examinations in spoken English 2004-2007.* (2nd ed.). London: Trinity College London.

Trinity College London. (2005b). *Integrated Skills in English examinations 0, I, II, III* (4th ed.). London: Trinity College London.

Tsui, A. B., & Fullilove, J. (1998). Bottom-up or top-down processing as a discriminator of L2 listening performance. *Applied Linguistics, 19*(4), 432-451.

Underwood, G., & Batt, V. (1996). *Reading and understanding: An introduction to the psychology of reading.* Cambridge, MA: Blackwell.

Weigle, S. C. (1999). Investigating rater / prompt interactions in writing assessment: Quantitative and qualitative approaches. *Assessing Writing, 6,* 145-178.

Weigle, S. C. (2002). *Assessing writing.* Cambridge: Cambridge University Press.

Weir, C. J. (2005). Limitations of the Common European Framework for developing comparable examinations and tests. *Language Testing, 22,* 281-300.

Wolfe, E. W. (2004). Identifying rater effects using latent trait models. *Psychology Science, 46,* 35-51.

Yi'an, W. (1998). What do tests of listening comprehension measure? A retrospection study of EFL test-takers performing a multiple-choice task. *Language Testing, 15,* 21-44.

Zieky, M., & Perie, M. (2006). *A primer on setting cut scores on tests of educational achievement.* Princeton, NJ: Educational Testing Service.

Appendices

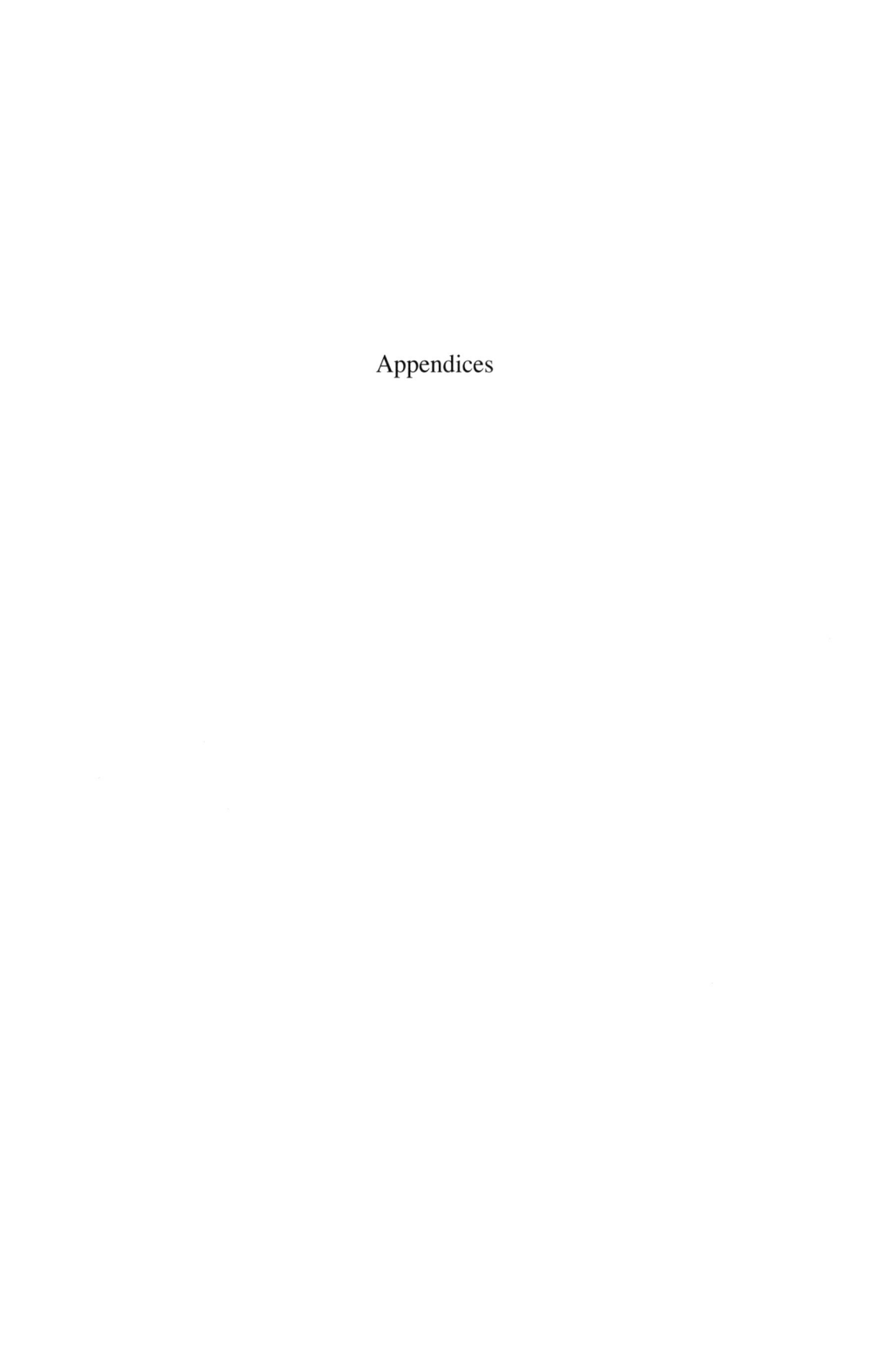

Thematic Glossary

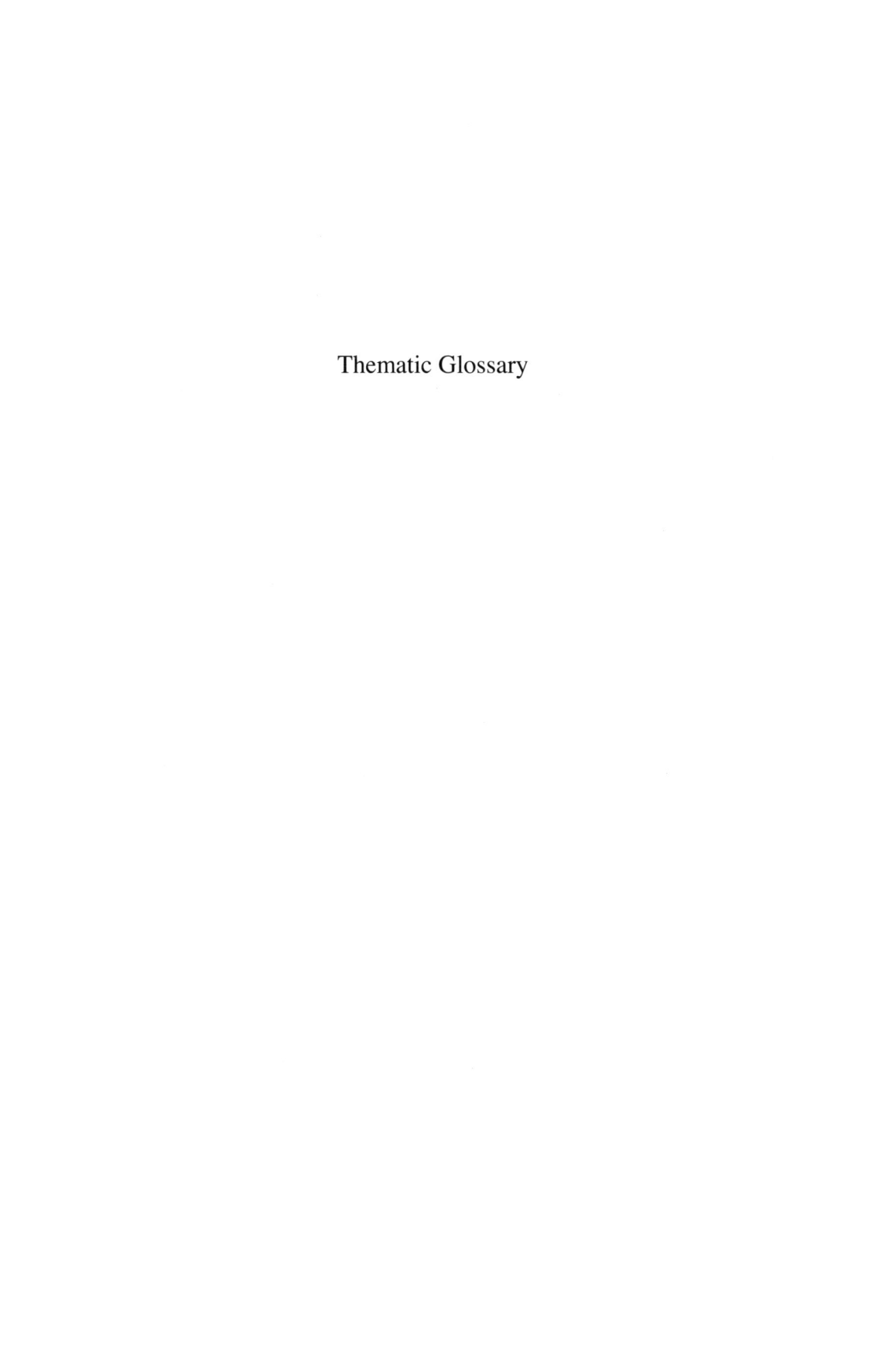

Booklet	A collection of items that is administered to an individual student. Typically, students in a single classroom received multiple booklets to minimize opportunities for cheating, which are linked via anchor items.
Item	A single question that is linked to a stimulus, which can be a graph, a text, or a picture.
Task / Testlet / Item bundle	A series of items that are connected by a common stimulus. Examples include reading passages with multiple items, graphics with multiple questions, and tables with multiple entries.
Prompt	The textual instruction that is provided for a writing section of a test.
Item Pool	The collection of all items that are stored in a database.
Anchor item	An item that is included in multiple booklets to link these booklets.
Dichotomous scores	Binary numbers assigned to student responses, typically '0' and '1' representing an "incorrect" and a "correct" response to a test question.
Polytomous scores	Graded scores assigned to student responses, typically '0', '1', '2', etc. representing degrees of acceptability of a response to a test question.
Scoring	The process of unambiguously assigning numbers to constructed responses of students based on a codebook that contains detailed information about the rules of assignment.
Rating	The process of assigning numbers to constructed responses of students based on a complex weighting of various descriptors of proficiency at each level. In contrast to coding, rating involves a judgment process.
Rater	A person who needs to be trained to provide ratings of written products.
Intra-rater reliability	The consistency of judgment (i.e., the scores) that is displayed by a single rater when he or she rates written products repeatedly over time.
Inter-rater reliability	The consistency of judgment (i.e., the scores) that is displayed by multiple raters when they rate the same written products at one point in time.
Paper-and-pencil test	A test that is printed on paper such that the test booklets are physical entities that are handed to the students, who respond to them by writing their answers in the booklets or on a separate answer sheet. The opposite of this are computer-based tests, which are electronically administered.

Speed test	A test for which there is a fixed time limit for responding, which might lead some students (e.g., less able, not focused) to miss some questions at the end of a section or a booklet. The opposite of this is power tests, which are designed to elicit the best possible performance of students without a time limit.
Criterion-referenced interpretation	An interpretation of test scores with regards to a certain performance level (i.e., criterion). For standards-based assessments, there are typically multiple criteria (i.e., proficiency levels) and, thus, multiple criterion-referenced interpretations. The opposite of this are criterion-referenced interpretations of test scores.
Norm-referenced interpretation	An interpretation of test scores with regards to an already existing distribution of test scores that has been established on a reference group (i.e., the norming group). Norm-referenced interpretations imply the rank-ordering of students and allow for gauging the developmental status of individuals. The opposite of this are criterion-referenced interpretations of test scores.
Balanced incomplete block design	A statistical design for administering a large number of items to a large number of students so that each student only responds to a subset of all items but all students can be statistically linked and results can be reported on a common proficiency scale.
Item response theory	A term from psychometrics that is used to collect a wide variety of statistical models that can be used to analyze data from questionnaires or achievement tests that target unobserved (i.e., latent) characteristics of subjects (e.g., students). The most commonly used model for analyzing item and learner characteristics in large-scale standards-based assessment is a Rasch model that can include explanatory variables, differential weights for different students, and complex scoring mechanisms.
Classical test theory	A term from psychometrics that is used to collect a series of statistical models that can be used to analyze data from questionnaires or achievement tests that target unobserved (i.e., latent) characteristics of subjects (e.g., students). Contrary to item response theory, classical test theory is less powerful in complex situations such as adaptive testing, optimal test design, and diagnostic testing, but provides useful indices for preliminary analyses of item functioning. Common indices associated with classical test theory include the item difficulty or p-value, the item discrimination or point-biserial / biserial correlation, and various reliability indices such as Cronbach's α.

Sample (Random & Convenient)	A subset of a larger collection of individuals or units, which is known as the population. In large-scale standards-based assessments, the most important samples are student samples and item samples. For inferences from samples to the populations from which they were drawn to be most powerful, the samples should be large, representative, and random. The more these characteristics are weakened, the weaker the sample-based inferences about the population will be.
Population	The collection of individuals or units to whom a generalization is desired and from whom a subset, a sample, is drawn to make such inferences. In large-scale standards-based assessments, the most important populations are students and item pools.
Psychometrics	A term commonly used in conjunction with statistics to denote a set of methodologies that allow researchers to analyze data from questionnaires or tests that are used to make inferences about unobserved (i.e., latent) characteristics of individuals (e.g., students). While psychometric models are statistical models, the term psychometric model is commonly used to refer to models with latent variables that are the focus of an analysis such as models in classical test theory or item response theory.
Proficiency scale	A single (i.e., unidimensional) ruler that allows for the comparison of individuals by rank-ordering them. Proficiency scales are typically continuous scales defined on the entire real number line. However, practically, most proficiency scores of individuals will fall within a limited range of this scale (e.g., -4 and +4 for many common item response theory models) and can be converted to any arbitrary scale with a different middle point and spread.
Proficiency level	A category that is created on a continuous proficiency scale by two cut-scores at the lower and upper end.
Standard-setting	A term that refers to a wide variety of consensual approaches that are used to have committees of experts set cut-scores on continuous proficiency scales. Since there are no "natural" or "true" cut-scores on these scales (i.e., since the scales are discretized), different methods combine different types of information, different types of judgment tasks, and different interaction processes to help experts reach a consensus on where the cut-scores should be set.

Cut-score	A score on a continuous scale that is used to mark the boundary between two theoretically defined levels of proficiency. Cut-scores are set not as a statistical necessity – in fact, the classifications they entail result in a statistical loss of precision – but as a means to facilitate reports about proficiency distributions that can be more easily communicated to a wide variety of stakeholders.
Stakeholder	Any person that uses a test-score to make decisions on its basis (e.g., teachers, parents, students, policy makers).

Appendix A:
Sample Grids from CEF

Table A1
Common Reference Levels: Global Scale

Proficient User	C2	Can understand with ease virtually everything heard or read. Can summarize information from different spoken or written sources, reconstructing arguments and accounts in a coherent presentation. Can express him/herself spontaneously, very fluently, and precisely, differentiating finer shades of meaning in more complex situations.
	C1	Can understand a wide range of demanding, longer texts, and recognise implicit meaning. Can express him/herself fluently and spontaneously without much obvious searching for expressions. Can use language flexibly and effectively for social, academic and professional purposes. Can produce clear, well-structured, detailed text on complex subjects, showing controlled use of organisational patterns, connectors and cohesive devices.
Independent User	B2	Can understand the main ideas of complex text on both concrete and abstract topics, including technical discussions in his/her field of specialisation. Can interact with a degree of fluency and spontaneity that makes regular interaction with native speakers quite possible without strain for either party. Can produce clear, detailed text on a wide range of subjects and explain a viewpoint in a topical issue giving the advantages and disadvantages of various options.
	B1	Can understand the main points of clear standard input on familiar matters regularly encountered in work, school, leisure, etc. Can deal with most situations likely to arise whilst travelling in an area where the language is spoken. Can produce simple connected text on topics which are familiar or of personal interest. Can describe experiences and events, dreams, hopes, and ambitions and briefly give reasons and explanations of opinions and plans.
Basic User	A2	Can understand sentences and frequently used expressions related to areas of most immediate relevance (e.g., very basic personal and family information, shopping, local geography, employment). Can communicate in simple and routine tasks requiring a simple and direct exchange of information on familiar and routine matters. Can describe in simple terms aspects of his/her background, immediate environment and matters of immediate need.
	A1	Can understand and use familiar everyday expressions and very basic phrases aimed at the satisfaction of needs of a concrete type. Can introduce him/herself and others and can ask and answer questions about personal details such as where he/she lives, people he/she knows and things he/she has. Can interact in a simple way provided the other person talks slowly and clearly an is prepared to help.

from: CEF, page 24.

Table A2
Common Reference Levels: Self-assessment Grid for Reading Comprehension

Level	Reading Comprehension
C2	I can red with ease virtually all forms of the written language, including abstract, structurally or linguistically complex texts such as manuals, specialised articles, and literary works.
C1	I can understand long and complex factual and literary texts, appreciating the distinctions of style. I can understand specialized articles and longer technical instructions, even when they do not related to my field.
B2	I can read articles and reports concerned with contemporary problems in which the writers adopt particular attitudes or viewpoints. I can understand contemporary literary prose.
B1	I can understand texts that consist mainly of high frequency everyday or job related language. I can understand the description of events, feelings, and wishes in personal letters.
A2	I can read very short, simple texts. I can find specific, predictable information in simple, everyday material such as advertisements, prospectuses, menus, and timetables and I can understand short simple personal letters.
A1	I can understand familiar names, words, and very simple sentences, for example on notices and posters or in catalogues.

from: CEF, pp. 26-27.

Table A3
Common Reference Levels: Self-assessment Grid for Listening Comprehension

Level	Listening Comprehension
C2	I have no difficulty in understanding any kind of spoken language, whether live or broadcast, even when delivered at fast native speed, provided I have some time to get familiar with the accent.
C1	I can understand extended speech even when it is not clearly structured and when relationships are only implied and not signalled explicitly. I can understand television programmes and films without too much effort.
B2	I can understand extended speech and lectures and follow even complex lines of argument provided the topic is reasonably familiar. I can understand most TV news and current affair programmes. I can understand the majority of films in standard dialect.
B1	I can understand the main points of clear standard speech on family matters regularly encountered in work, school, leisure, etc. I can understand the main point of many radio or TV programmes on current affairs or topics of personal or professional interest when the delivery is relatively slow and clear.
A2	I can understand phrases and the highest frequency vocabulary related to areas of most immediate personal relevance (e.g., very basic personal and family information, shopping, local areas, employment). I can catch the main point in short, clear, simple messages and announcements.
A1	I recognize familiar words and very basic phrases concerning myself, my family and immediate concrete surroundings when people speak slowly and clearly.

from: CEF, pp. 26-27.

Table A4
Common Reference Levels: Self-assessment Grid for Writing

Level	Writing
C2	I can write clear, smoothly flowing text in an appropriate style. I can write complex letters, reports or articles which present a case with an effective logical structure which helps the recipient to notice and remember significant points. I can write summaries and reviews of professional or literary works.
C1	I can express myself in clear, well-structured text, expressing points of view at some length. I can write about complex subjects in a letter, an essay or a report, underlining what I consider to be the salient issues. I can select style appropriate to the reader in mind.
B2	I can write clear, detailed text on a wide range of subjects related to my interests. I can write an essay or report, passing on information or giving reasons in support of or against a particular point of view. I can write letters highlighting the personal significance of events and experiences.
B1	I can write simple connected text on topics which are familiar or of personal interest. I can write personal letters describing experiences and impressions.
A2	I can write short, simple notes and messages relating to matters in areas of immediate need. I can write a very simple personal letter, for example thanking someone for something.
A1	I can write a short, simple postcard, for example sending holiday greetings. I can fill in forms with personal details, for example entering my name, nationality and address on a hotel registration form.

from: CEF, pp. 26-27.

Appendix B:
National Educational Standards for English as a First Foreign Language

Table B1
Competences in the NES for Listening and Aural-visual Comprehension

	Die Schülerinnen und Schüler können Wendungen und Wörter verstehen, wenn es um Dinge von ganz unmittelbarer Bedeutung geht (z. B. ganz grundlegende Informationen zu Person, Familie, Einkaufen, Schule, näherer Umgebung), sofern deutlich und langsam gesprochen wird (A2).	
Hör- und Hör-/ Sehverstehen (Hauptschulabschluss)	*Die Schülerinnen und Schüler können ...*	
	1.1	im Allgemeinen das Thema von Gesprächen, die in ihrer Gegenwart geführt werden, erkennen, wenn langsam und deutlich gesprochen wird (A2),
	1.2	das Wesentliche von kurzen, klaren und einfachen Durchsagen und Mitteilungen erfassen (A2),
	1.3	die Hauptinformationen von kurzen, langsam und deutlich gesprochenen Tonaufnahmen über vorhersehbare alltägliche Dinge entnehmen (A2) sowie die Hauptinformationen von Fernsehmeldungen über Ereignisse erfassen, wenn der Kommentar durch das Bild unterstützt wird (A2+).
Hör- und Hör-/ Sehverstehen (Mittlerer Abschluss)	*Die Schülerinnen und Schüler können unkomplizierte Sachinformationen über gewöhnliche alltags- oder berufsbezogene Themen verstehen und dabei die Hauptaussagen und Einzelinformationen erkennen, wenn in deutlich artikulierter Standardsprache gesprochen wird (B1+).*	
	Die Schülerinnen und Schüler können ...	
	1.4	im Allgemeinen den Hauptpunkten von längeren Gesprächen folgen, die in ihrer Gegenwart geführt werden (B1),
	1.5	Vorträge verstehen, wenn die Thematik vertraut und die Darstellung unkompliziert und klar strukturiert ist (B1+),
	1.6	Ankündigungen und Mitteilungen zu konkreten Themen verstehen, die in normaler Geschwindigkeit in Standardsprache gesprochen werden (B2),
	1.7	vielen Filmen folgen, deren Handlung im Wesentlichen durch Bild und Aktion getragen wird (B1),
	1.8	in Radionachrichten und in einfacheren Tonaufnahmen über vertraute Themen die Hauptpunkte verstehen, wenn relativ langsam und deutlich gesprochen wird (B1),
	1.9	das Wesentliche von Fernsehsendungen zu vertrauten Themen verstehen, sofern darin relativ langsam und deutlich gesprochen wird (B1).

Table B2
Competences in the NES for Reading Comprehension

	Die Schülerinnen und Schüler können kurze, einfache Texte lesen und verstehen, die einen sehr frequenten Wortschatz und einen gewissen Anteil international bekannter Wörter enthalten (A2).	
Leseverstehen (Hauptschul-abschluss)	*Die Schülerinnen und Schüler können …*	
	2.1	kurze, einfache persönliche Briefe und E-Mails verstehen (A2),
	2.2	konkrete, voraussagbare Informationen in einfachen Alltagstexten auffinden, z. B. in Anzeigen, Prospekten, Speisekarten, Fahrplänen, Programmzeitschriften (A2),
	2.3	gebräuchliche Zeichen und Schilder an öffentlichen Orten, z. B. Wegweiser, Warnungen vor Gefahr verstehen (A2),
	2.4	aus einfacheren schriftlichen Materialien wie Briefen, Broschüren, Zeitungsartikeln (oder auch dem Niveau entsprechenden fiktionalen Texten) spezifische Informationen herausfinden (A2),
	2.5	einfache Anleitungen für Apparate verstehen, mit denen sie im Alltag zu tun haben (A2).
	Die Schülerinnen und Schüler können verschiedene unkomplizierte Texte aus Themenfeldern ihres Interessen- und Erfahrungsbereiches lesen und verstehen (B1).	
Leseverstehen (Mittlerer Abschluss)	*Die Schülerinnen und Schüler können …*	
	2.6	Korrespondenz lesen, die sich auf das eigene Interessengebiet bezieht und die wesentliche Aussage erfassen (B2),
	2.7	klar formulierte Anweisungen, unkomplizierte Anleitungen, Hinweise und Vorschriften verstehen (B1/ B2),
	2.8	längere Texte nach gewünschten Informationen durchsuchen und Informationen aus verschiedenen Texten zusammentragen, um eine bestimmte Aufgabe zu lösen (B1+),
	2.9	in kürzeren literarischen Texten (z. B. Short Stories) die wesentlichen Aussagen erfassen und diese zusammentragen, um eine bestimmte Aufgabe zu lösen (B1),
	2.10	die Aussagen einfacher literarischer Texte verstehen,
	2.11	in klar geschriebenen argumentativen Texten zu vertrauten Themen die wesentlichen Schlussfolgerungen erkennen, z. B. in Zeitungsartikeln (B1/ B1+).

Table B3
Competences in the NES for Speaking

Sprechen: An Gesprächen teilnehmen (Hauptschulabschluss)	\multicolumn{2}{l}{*Die Schülerinnen und Schüler können sich in einfachen, routinemäßigen Situationen verständigen, in denen es um einen unkomplizierten und direkten Austausch von Informationen über vertraute Themen geht (A2).*}
	\multicolumn{2}{l}{*Die Schülerinnen und Schüler können ...*}
	3.1	alltägliche Höflichkeitsformeln verwenden, um jemanden zu begrüßen oder anzusprechen (A2),
	3.2	jemanden einladen und auf Einladungen reagieren (A2),
	3.3	um Entschuldigung bitten und auf Entschuldigungen reagieren (A2),
	3.4	sagen, was sie gern haben und was nicht (A2),
	3.5	auf einfache Weise praktische Fragen des Alltags besprechen und Verabredungen treffen, wenn sie klar, langsam und direkt angesprochen werden (A2),
	3.6	sich in einfachen Routinesituationen (Einkaufen, Essen, öffentliche Verkehrsmittel) verständigen und Informationen geben und erfragen (A2),
	3.7	mit Formulierungshilfen die eigene Meinung zu lebenspraktischen Fragestellungen äußern, wenn diese Fragen ggf. in Kernpunkten wiederholt werden,
	3.8	in einem Interview einfache Fragen beantworten und auf einfache Feststellungen reagieren (A2).
Sprechen: An Gesprächen teilnehmen (Mittlerer Abschluss)	\multicolumn{2}{l}{*Die Schülerinnen und Schüler können an Gesprächen über vertraute Themen teilnehmen, persönliche Meinungen ausdrücken und Informationen austauschen (B1).*}
	\multicolumn{2}{l}{*Die Schülerinnen und Schüler können ...*}
	3.9	soziale Kontakte herstellen durch Begrüßung, Abschied, Sich-Vorstellen, Danken und Höflichkeitsformeln verwenden (A2),
	3.10	Gefühle wie Überraschung, Freude, Trauer, Interesse und Gleichgültigkeit ausdrücken und auf entsprechende Gefühlsäußerungen reagieren (B1),
	3.11	ein Gespräch oder eine Diskussion beginnen, fortführen und auch bei sprachlichen Schwierigkeiten aufrechterhalten (B1),
	3.12	die meisten Dienstleistungsgespräche und routinemäßigen Situationen bewältigen, z. B. Umgang mit öffentlichen Einrichtungen während eines Auslandsaufenthaltes, Einkauf, Essen (B1),
	3.13	in einem Interview konkrete Auskünfte geben, z. B. in Bewerbungsgesprächen (B1+),
	3.14	eine kurze Geschichte, einen Artikel, einen Vortrag, ein Interview oder eine Dokumentarsendung zu vertrauten Themen einem Gesprächspartner vorstellen und Informationsfragen dazu beantworten (B1+),
	3.15	in Gesprächen und Diskussionen kurz zu den Standpunkten anderer Stellung nehmen und höflich Überzeugungen und Meinungen, Zustimmung und Ablehnung ausdrücken (B1/ B1+).

Sprechen: Zusammenhängendes Sprechen (Hauptschulabschluss)	*Die Schülerinnen und Schüler können eine einfache Beschreibung von Menschen, Lebens-, Schul- oder Arbeitsbedingungen, Alltagsroutinen, Vorlieben oder Abneigungen usw. geben und zwar in kurzen, einfach strukturierten Wendungen und Sätzen (A2).*
	Die Schülerinnen und Schüler können … 3.16 eine kurze, einfache Präsentation zu einem vertrauten Thema geben (A2), 3.17 etwas erzählen und in Form einer einfachen Aufzählung berichten (A2), 3.18 kurz und einfach über eine Tätigkeit oder ein Ereignis berichten (A2).
Sprechen: Zusammenhängendes Sprechen (Mittlerer Abschluss)	*Die Schülerinnen und Schüler können Erfahrungen und Sachverhalte zusammenhängend darstellen, z. B. beschreiben, berichten, erzählen und bewerten (B1).*
	Die Schülerinnen und Schüler können … 3.19 mit einfachen Mitteln Gegenstände und Vorgänge des Alltags beschreiben, z. B. Rezepte, Wegbeschreibungen, Spielregeln, Bedienungsanleitungen (A2), 3.20 eine vorbereitete Präsentation zu einem vertrauten Thema vortragen, wobei die Hauptpunkte hinreichend präzise erläutert werden (B1), 3.21 für Ansichten, Pläne oder Handlungen kurze Begründungen oder Erklärungen geben (B1).

Table B4
Competences in the NES for Writing

Schreiben (Hauptschulabschluss)	*Die Schülerinnen und Schüler können in einer Reihe einfacher Sätze über die eigene Familie, die Lebensumstände und die Schule schreiben. Sie können eine sehr kurze, elementare Beschreibung von Ereignissen, Handlungen, Plänen und persönlichen Erfahrungen erstellen sowie kurze Geschichten nach sprachlichen Vorgaben verfassen (A2/A2+).*
	Die Schülerinnen und Schüler können ...
	4.1 kurze, einfache Notizen und Mitteilungen schreiben, die sich auf unmittelbare Bedürfnisse und notwendige Dinge beziehen (A2),
	4.2 einfache, persönliche Briefe und E-Mails schreiben (A2),
	4.3 nach sprachlichen Vorgaben kurze einfache Texte (Berichte, Beschreibungen, Geschichten, Gedichte) verfassen (A2).
Schreiben (Mittlerer Abschluss)	*Die Schülerinnen und Schüler können zusammenhängende Texte zu vertrauten Themen aus ihrem Interessengebiet verfassen (B1).*
	Die Schülerinnen und Schüler können ...
	4.4 eine Nachricht notieren, wenn jemand nach Informationen fragt oder ein Problem erläutert (B1+),
	4.4 In persönlichen Briefen Mitteilungen, einfache Informationen und Gedanken darlegen (B1),
	4.6 einfache standardisierte Briefe und E-Mails adressatengerecht formulieren, z. B. Anfragen, Bewerbungen (B1),
	4.7 unkomplizierte, detaillierte Texte zu einer Reihe verschiedener Themen aus ihren Interessengebieten verfassen, z. B. Erfahrungsberichte, Geschichten, Beschreibungen (B1),
	4.8 kurze einfache Aufsätze zu Themen von allgemeinem Interesse schreiben (B1),
	4.9 kurze Berichte zu vertrauten Themen schreiben, darin Informationen weitergeben, Gründe für Handlungen angeben und Stellung nehmen (B 1+).

Table B5
Competences in the NES for Language Mediation

Sprachmittlung (Hauptschulabschluss)	5.1 Die Schülerinnen und Schüler können mündlich einfache sprachliche Äußerungen von der einen in die andere Sprache sinngemäß übertragen.
Sprachmittlung (Mittlerer Abschluss)	*Die Schülerinnen und Schüler können mündlich in Routinesituationen und schriftlich zu vertrauten Themen zusammenhängende sprachliche Äußerungen und Texte sinngemäß von der einen in die andere Sprache übertragen.* *Die Schülerinnen und Schüler können ...* 5.2 in Alltagssituationen sprachmittelnd agieren, 5.3 persönliche und einfache Sach- und Gebrauchstexte sinngemäß übertragen.

Table B6
Competences in the NES for Vocabulary

Wortschatz (Hauptschulabschluss)	6.1 Die Schülerinnen und Schüler verfügen über einen elementaren Wortschatz, der sich aus vertrauten Themen entwickelt hat, hochfrequente und vielseitig verwendbare Einheiten einschließt und für die Bewältigung elementarer Kommunikationsbedürfnisse in vertrauten Situationen hinreichend ist. Die rezeptive Verfügbarkeit geht über die produktive Anwendung hinaus.
Wortschatz (Mittlerer Abschluss)	6.2 Die Schülerinnen und Schüler verfügen über einen hinreichend großen Wortschatz, um sich mit Hilfe von einigen Umschreibungen über die häufigsten Alltagsthemen der eigenen und der fremdsprachlichen Gesellschaft und Kultur (vgl. Kapitel 3.3) äußern zu können. Darüber hinaus sind sie in der Lage, zusätzliche lexikalische Einheiten hörend oder lesend zu verstehen (rezeptiver Wortschatz) oder selbstständig aus Texten zu erschließen (potentieller Wortschatz). Die Schülerinnen und Schüler machen aber noch elementare Fehler, wenn es darum geht, komplexere Sachverhalte auszudrücken und wenig vertraute Themen und Situationen zu bewältigen.

Table B7
Competences in the NES for Grammar

Grammatik (Hauptschul- abschluss)	*Die Schülerinnen und Schüler können einfache Strukturen intentions- und situationsangemessen verwenden, machen aber noch elementare Fehler. Trotzdem wird in der Regel klar, was sie zum Ausdruck bringen möchten. Die Reichweite der rezeptiv verfügbaren Strukturen ist erheblich größer als die der produktiv verfügbaren Strukturen.*	
	Sie können unter anderem …	
	7.1	Aussagen, Fragen und Aufforderungen in bejahter und verneinter Form verstehen und formulieren,
	7.2	einfache Handlungen, Ereignisse und Sachverhalte als gegenwärtig, vergangen oder zukünftig erkennen und wiedergeben,
	7.3	räumliche, zeitliche und logische Beziehungen erkennen und durch einfache Strukturen herstellen,
	7.4	Handlungsperspektiven (Bedingungsgefüge und passive Satzkonstruktionen) verstehen,
	7.5	Anzahl, Art und Zugehörigkeit von Gegenständen, Lebewesen und Sachverhalten erkennen und mit elementaren sprachlichen Mitteln beschreiben.
Grammatik (Mittlerer Abschluss)	*Die Schülerinnen und Schüler verfügen im Allgemeinen über verwendungshäufige grammatische Strukturen, können diese intentions- und situationsangemessen anwenden und haben ein elementares Strukturbewusstsein entwickelt. Sie machen zwar noch Fehler, aber es bleibt klar, was sie zum Ausdruck bringen möchten. Darüber hinaus können sie ein Repertoire von häufig verwendeten Redefloskeln und von Wendungen ausreichend korrekt verwenden. Die Reichweite der rezeptiv verfügbaren Strukturen ist größer als die der produktiv verfügbaren Strukturen.*	
	Sie können unter anderem …	
	7.6	Aussagen, Fragen und Aufforderungen in bejahter und verneinter Form verstehen und formulieren,
	7.7	Handlungen, Ereignisse und Sachverhalte als gegenwärtig, vergangen, zukünftig oder zeitlos, mehrere Geschehnisse als gleichzeitig oder aufeinander folgend bzw. unter Berücksichtigung von Vor- und Nachzeitigkeit erkennen und wiedergeben,
	7.8	räumliche, zeitliche und logische Beziehungen erkennen und herstellen,
	7.9	Handlungsperspektiven (aktive und passive Satzkonstruktionen) verstehen und selbst formulieren,
	7.10	Anzahl, Art und Zugehörigkeit von Gegenständen, Lebewesen und Sachverhalten erkennen und beschreiben,
	7.11	Informationen wörtlich und vermittelt wiedergeben (direkte / indirekte Rede),
	7.12	Bedingungen und Bezüge formulieren.

Table B8
Competences in the NES for Quality of Speech

Aussprache und Intonation (Hauptschulabschluss)	*Die Schülerinnen und Schüler ...*
	8.1 beherrschen die Aussprache im Allgemeinen klar genug, um verstanden zu werden; manchmal wird eine Wiederholung erforderlich,
	8.2 nutzen Zeichen der Lautschrift als Aussprachehilfe,
	8.3 können elementare Intonationsmuster anwenden.
Aussprache und Intonation (Mittlerer Abschluss)	*Die Schülerinnen und Schüler ...*
	8.4 können verschiedenartige Aussprachevarianten der Zielsprache verstehen,
	8.5 beherrschen die Aussprache in der Weise, dass diese in der Regel weder auf der Wort- noch auf der Satzebene zu Missverständnissen führt,
	8.6 können die Zeichen der Lautschrift sprachlich umsetzen.

Table B9
Competences in the NES for Orthography

Orthographie (Hauptschulabschluss)	9.1	Die Schüler können die Redemittel eines grundlegenden Repertoires schriftlich verständlich wiedergeben.
Orthographie (Mittlerer Abschluss)	9.2	Die Schüler können unter Anwendung der Rechtschreib- und Zeichensetzungsregeln der Zielsprache ausreichend korrekt und verständlich schreiben.

Table B10
Intercultural Competences in the NES

Interkulturelle Kompetenzen umfassen mehr als Wissen und mehr als eine Technik. Sie umfassen auch und vor allem Haltungen, die ihren Ausdruck gleichermaßen im Denken, Fühlen und Handeln und ihre Verankerung in entsprechenden Lebenserfahrungen und ethischen Prinzipien haben. Interkulturelle Kompetenzen beinhalten Einsicht in die Kulturabhängigkeit des eigenen Denkens, Handelns und Verhaltens sowie die Fähigkeit und Bereitschaft zur Wahrnehmung und Analyse fremdkultureller Perspektiven.		
Interkulturelle Kompetenz (Hauptschulabschluss)		*Die Schülerinnen und Schüler ...*
	10.1	kennen elementare spezifische Kommunikations- und Interaktionsregeln ausgewählter englisch- bzw. französischsprachiger Länder und können in vertrauten Situationen sprachlich angemessen handeln,
	10.2	kennen gängige Sicht- und Wahrnehmungsweisen, Vorurteile und Stereotype des eigenen und des fremdkulturellen Landes und setzen sich mit ihnen auseinander,
	10.3	sind neugierig auf Fremdes, aufgeschlossen für andere Kulturen und akzeptieren kulturelle Vielfalt ohne Angst und Vorbehalte,
	10.4	sind bereit, ungewohnte Erfahrungen auszuhalten, sich auf fremde Situationen einzustellen und sich in Situationen des Alltagslebens angemessen zu verhalten,
	10.5	können sich in Bezug auf die Befindlichkeiten und Denkweisen in fremdkulturelle Personen hineinversetzen,
	10.6	können Missverständnisse und Konfliktsituationen erkennen und versuchen, diese mit den ihnen zur Verfügung stehenden sprachlichen Mitteln zu klären bzw. zur Klärung beizutragen.
Interkulturelle Kompetenz (Mittlerer Abschluss)		*Die Schülerinnen und Schüler ...*
	10.7	kennen elementare spezifische Kommunikations- und Interaktionsregeln ausgewählter englisch- bzw. französischsprachiger Länder und verfügen über ein entsprechendes Sprachregister, das sie in vertrauten Situationen anwenden können,
	10.8	sind neugierig auf Fremdes, aufgeschlossen für andere Kulturen und akzeptieren kulturelle Vielfalt,
	10.9	sind bereit, sich auf fremde Situationen einzustellen und sich in Situationen des Alltagslebens angemessen zu verhalten,
	10.10	sind in der Lage, ungewohnte Erfahrungen auszuhalten, mit ihnen sinnvoll und angemessen umzugehen und das Fremde nicht als etwas wahrzunehmen, das Angst macht,
	10.11	können sich in Bezug auf die Befindlichkeiten und Denkweisen in den fremdkulturellen Partner hineinversetzen,
	10.12	kennen gängige Sicht- und Wahrnehmungsweisen, Vorurteile und Stereotype des eigenen und des fremdkulturellen Landes und setzen sich mit ihnen auseinander,

	10.13	können kulturelle Differenzen, Missverständnisse und Konfliktsituationen bewusst wahrnehmen, sich darüber verständigen und gegebenenfalls gemeinsam handeln.
Interkulturelle Kompetenz (Beide Abschlüsse)		*Die Kenntnisse und Fertigkeiten beziehen sich insbesondere auf Charakteristika der eigenen und der fremdsprachlichen Gesellschaft und Kultur aus folgenden Bereichen*
	10.14	das tägliche Leben (Alltag, Schule und Freizeit, Essen und Trinken, Arbeitszeiten und -gewohnheiten, Feiertage u.a.),
	10.15	Lebensbedingungen (Lebensstandard, geografische, soziokulturelle Merkmale, u. a.),
	10.16	zwischenmenschliche Beziehungen (Geschlechterbeziehungen, Familienstrukturen, Generationsbeziehungen, u. a.),
	10.17	Werten, Normen, Überzeugungen, Einstellungen (u. a. in Bezug auf regionale Kulturen, Traditionen, Geschichte, Minderheiten, Kunst).

Table B11
Receptive Methodological Competences in the NES

Methodenkompetenz (Rezeption) (Hauptschulabschluss)		*Die Schülerinnen und Schüler können ...*
	11.1	verschiedene Hör- und Lesetechniken (u.a. globales, suchendes, detailliertes Hören und Lesen) aufgabenbezogen/funktionsbezogen einsetzen,
	11.2	Weitgehend eigenständig wesentliche Informationen festhalten durch Unterstreichen und farbliches Hervorheben, ordnende Randnotizen sowie das Notieren von Stichworten.
Methodenkompetenz (Rezeption) (Mittlerer Abschluss)		*Die Schülerinnen und Schüler können ...*
	11.3	verschiedene Hör- und Lesetechniken auf unterschiedliche Textarten (z. B. Sachtexte, Artikel, literarische Kleinformen) anwenden, sich schnell einen groben Überblick über den Inhalt eines Textes verschaffen,
	11.4	wichtige Details durch Unterstreichen markieren,
	11.5	wichtige Textstellen durch farbliches Hervorheben, durch das Notieren von Stichworten und durch ordnende ergänzende Randnotizen besonders kenntlich machen.

Table B12
Interactive Methodological Competences in the NES

	Die Schülerinnen und Schüler können ...
Methoden-kompetenz (Interaktion) (Hauptschul-abschluss)	12.6 in der Klasse und in Alltagssituationen Kontakt aufnehmen, auf Ansprache reagieren und sich in Kommunikationsprozesse einbringen, 12.7 grundlegende Regeln des Gesprächsablaufs beachten und Verständigungsprobleme durch Rückfragen und nonverbale Mittel überwinden, 12.8 einfache Techniken des Vermittelns zwischen zwei Sprachen einsetzen.
Methoden-kompetenz (Interaktion) (Mittlerer Abschluss)	*Die Schülerinnen und Schüler können ...* 12.9 sich in der Klasse, mit Partnern und in Gruppen in der Fremdsprache verständigen und Kommunikationsprozesse aufrecht erhalten, 12.10 sich in realen Alltagssituationen mit unterschiedlichen, englisch- bzw. französischsprachigen Personen verständigen und Verständigungsprobleme durch Rückfragen, durch Vereinfachungen, durch Höflichkeitsformeln und nonverbale Mittel überwinden, 12.11 Techniken des Vermittelns zwischen zwei Sprachen einsetzen.

Table B13
Productive Methodological Competences in the NES

Methoden- kompetenz (Textproduktion) (Hauptschul- abschluss)	*Die Schülerinnen und Schüler können ...*	
	13.1	sich Informationen aus Texten beschaffen und sie als Grundlage für die eigene Textproduktion verwenden,
	13.2	Techniken zur Vorbereitung eigener Texte oder Präsentationen anwenden, z. B. Stichworte notieren, Gliederungen erstellen, Handlungsgeländer anfertigen, Bilder verwenden,
	13.3	Texte unter Verwendung der vorbereiteten Hilfen mündlich vortragen oder schriftlich verfassen.
Methoden- kompetenz (Textproduktion) (Mittlerer Abschluss)	*Die Schülerinnen und Schüler können...*	
	13.4	sich Informationen aus unterschiedlichen fremdsprachlichen Textquellen beschaffen, diese vergleichen, auswählen und bearbeiten,
	13.5	Techniken des Notierens zur Vorbereitung eigener Texte oder Präsentationen nutzen,
	13.6	mit Hilfe von Stichworten, Gliederungen, Handlungsgeländern Texte mündlich vortragen oder schriftlich verfassen, die Phasen des Schreibprozesses (Entwerfen, Schreiben, Überarbeiten) selbstständig durchführen.

Table B14
Learning Strategies in the NES

Lernstrategien beziehen sich hier auf den Erwerb und den Einsatz sprachlicher Mittel, d.h. auf Aussprache, Intonation, Orthographie, Wortschatz sowie auf Grammatik.		
Lernstrategien (Hauptschul- abschluss)	*Die Schülerinnen und Schüler können ...*	
	14.1	Hilfsmittel zum Nachschlagen wie Wörterbücher, grammatische Erklärungen und andere Lernhilfen nutzen,
	14.2	Verfahren zum Memorieren und Abrufen von Wörtern und Redemitteln anwenden.
Lernstrategien (Mittlerer Abschluss)	*Die Schülerinnen und Schüler können ...*	
	14.3	Hilfsmittel zum Nachschlagen und Lernen, z. B. Wörterbücher, Grammatikbücher usw. selbstständig nutzen,
	14.4	Verfahren zur Vernetzung, Strukturierung, Memorierung und Speicherung von sprachlichen Inputs, z. B. von Wortschatz, anwenden.

Table B15
Competences in the NES for Presentation and New Media

Präsentation und Neue Medien (Hauptschulabschluss)	|	*Die Schülerinnen und Schüler können ...*
	15.1	Neue Medien zur Informationsbeschaffung, zur kommunikativen Interaktion und zum Lernen einsetzen,
	15.2	Präsentationstechniken zur Darstellung von Arbeitsergebnissen einsetzen (Medien auswählen, Gliederungs- und Visualisierungstechniken anwenden).
Präsentation und Neue Medien (Mittlerer Abschluss)		*Die Schülerinnen und Schüler können ...*
	15.3	Präsentationstechniken einsetzen (Medienwahl, Gliederungstechniken, Visualisierungstechniken, Gruppenpräsentation),
	15.4	mit Lernprogrammen (auch Multimedia) arbeiten,
	15.5	Neue Technologien zur Informationsbeschaffung, zur kommunikativen Interaktion (E-Mail) und zur Präsentation der Ergebnisse nutzen.

Table B16
Methodological Competences in the NES for Self-regulated Learning

Lernorganisation und Lernbewusstheit (Hauptschulabschluss)		*Die Schülerinnen und Schüler können ...*
	16.1	selbstständig und kooperativ arbeiten,
	16.2	Methoden der Projektarbeit (Planung, Durchführung, Auswertung) anwenden,
	16.3	für sie förderliche Lernbedingungen erkennen und nutzen, ihre Lernarbeit organisieren und die Zeit einteilen,
	16.4	ihren eigenen Lernfortschritt ggf. in einem Portfolio dokumentieren,
	16.5	den Nutzen der Fremdsprache für persönliche und berufliche Kontakte einschätzen.
Lernorganisation und Lernbewusstheit (Mittlerer Abschluss)		*Die Schülerinnen und Schüler können ...*
	16.6	den Nutzen der Fremdsprache zur Pflege von persönlichen und beruflichen Kontakten einschätzen,
	16.7	selbstständig, mit einem Partner oder in Gruppen längere Zeit arbeiten,
	16.8	ausgewählte Projekte (z. B. bilinguale Projekte) bearbeiten,
	16.9	für sie förderliche Lernbedingungen erkennen und nutzen, ihre Lernarbeit organisieren und die Zeit einteilen,
	16.10	Fehler erkennen und diese Erkenntnisse für den eigenen Lernprozess nutzen,
	16.11	ihren eigenen Lernfortschritt beschreiben und ggf. in einem Portfolio dokumentieren,
	16.12	Methoden des Spracherwerbs reflektieren und diese auf das Lernen weiterer Sprachen übertragen.

Appendix C:
Construct Definitions in the CEF,
the NES, and other Large-scale Assessments

Table C1
General and Communicative Language Competences in the CEF with Associated Scales

Level 1	Level 2	Level 3	Scales
General competences	Declarative knowledge (savoir)	Knowledge of the world	---
		Sociocultural knowledge	---
		Intercultural awareness	---
	Skills and know-how (savoir-faire)	Practical skills and know-how	---
		Intercultural skills and know-how	---
	Existential knowledge (savoir-être)	---	---
	Ability to learn (savoir-apprendre)	Language and communication awareness	---
		General phonetic awareness and skills	---
		Study skills	---
		Heuristic skills	---
Communicative language competences	Linguistic competences	General	110
		Lexical competence	112
		Grammatical competence	114
		Semantic competence	---
		Phonological competence	117
		Orthographic competence	118
		Orthoepic competence	---
	Sociolinguistic competence	General	122
		Linguistic markers of social relations	---
		Politeness conventions	---
		Expressions of folk wisdom	---
		Register differences	---
		Dialect and accent	---
	Pragmatic competences	Discourse competence	124–125
		Functional competence	129

Table C2
Communicative Language Activities, Strategies, and Processes in the CEF with Associated Scales

Level 1	Level 2	Level 3	Scale
Communicative language activities and strategies	Productive activities and strategies	Oral production (speaking)	58–60
		Written production (writing)	61–62
		Production strategies	64–65
	Receptive activities and strategies	Aural reception (listening comprehension)	66–68
		Visual reception (reading comprehension)	69–71
		Audio-visual reception	71
		Reception strategies	72
	Interactive activities and strategies	Spoken interaction	74–82
		Written interaction	83–84
		Face-to-face interaction	---
		Man-machine communication	---
		Interaction strategies	86–87
	Mediating activities and strategies	Oral mediation	---
		Written mediation	---
		Mediation strategies	---
	Non-verbal communication	Practical actions	---
		Paralinguistics	---
		Paratextual features	---
Communicative language processes	Planning	---	---
	Execution	Production	---
		Reception	---
		Interaction	---
	Monitoring	---	---

Table C3

Types of Reading Comprehension Competencies in the NES

NES – HSA (2004)	*Learners can …* 1. understand short, simple, personal letters and e-mails, 2. find concrete, predictable information in simple everyday texts, (e. g. in adverts, leaflets, menus, timetables, programme magazines), 3. understand common signs and signboards in public places (e.g., direction signs, danger warnings), 4. find specific information in simple written materials (e.g., letters, leaflets, newspaper articles, fiction), 5. understand manuals for devices used in their everyday lives.	Reading comprehension is the ability to read and understand short, simple texts with a very common vocabulary and a certain level of internationally known words (A2).	All students obtaining a *Hauptschulabschluss*.
NES – MA (2003)	*Learners can …* 1. understand the main information in correspondence relating to their own sphere of interest, 2. understand clearly stated and straightforward instructions, directions and regulations, 3. search longer texts for required information to solve a particular task, 4. gather information from several texts to solve a particular task, 5. capture the main information in shorter literary texts (e. g. short stories) and collating it to solve a particular task, 6. understand the messages of simple fictional texts, 7. recognize the main conclusions in clearly written, argumentative texts on familiar topics (e .g. newspaper articles).	Reading comprehension is the ability to largely read independently and to understand different texts from familiar subject areas (B1+).	All students obtaining a *Mittlerer Abschluss*.

Note. HSA – Hauptschulabschluss, MSA – Mittlerer Schulabschluss.

Table C4
Types of Reading Comprehension Competencies in Large-scale Assessments

Study	Types or Reading	Construct Definition	Population
PISA (2000 / 2003) LISA (2003)	1. Retrieving information 2. Forming a broad understanding 3. Developing an interpretation 4. Reflecting on the content of a text 5. Reflecting on the form of a text	PISA measures students' applied ability to deal with written material through handling different kinds of text and performing different types of reading tasks in relation to various situations where reading is needed. (OECD, 2004, p. 272)	All 15-year old students attending educational institutions. (OECD, 2002, p. 39)
PIRLS (2001 / 2006)	1. Focusing on and retrieving explicitly stated information 2. Making straight-forward inferences 3. Interpreting and integrating ideas and information 4. Examining and evaluating content, language, and textual elements	Reading literacy is the ability to understand and use those written language forms required by society and / or valued by the individual. Young readers can construct meaning from a variety of texts. They read to learn, to participate in communities of readers in school and everyday life, and for enjoyment. (IEA, 2006, p. 3)	All students in 4th grade, counting from the first year of ISCED level 1. (IEA, 2006, p. 7)
DESI (2004)	1. Understanding specific information 2. Integrating pieces of information to understand the main ideas 3. Interpreting text	Reading comprehension is the ability to connect explicitly and implicitly presented information in narrative texts with world knowledge commensurate with curricular exposure to perform different types of reading tasks. This is done by inferring unknown linguistic elements from context and integrating pieces of information to form coherent mental representations of parts of texts and entire texts. (see DESI Consortium, 2006, p. 19)	All students in 9th grade in *allgemein bildenden Schulen*. (DESI Consortium, 2006, p. 3)

Table C5
Types of Listening Comprehension Competencies in the NES

	Learners can …	The learners can understand phrases and words related to areas of most immediate relevance (e. g. very basic personal and family information, shopping, school, immediate environment), if expressed clearly and slowly (A2).	All students obtaining a *Hauptschulabschluss*.
NES – HSA (2004)	1. generally recognize the subject of conversations in their presence, if the participants speak slowly and clearly (A2), 2. understand the main points of short, clear and simple announcements and messages (A2), 3. understand the main information in short audio recordings on predictable everyday topics if spoken slowly and clearly (A2) and understand the main information in television programmes, if the commentary is supported by images (A2+).		
NES – MA (2003)	*Learners can…* 1. generally follow the main points of longer conversations in present tense (B1), 2. understand straightforward, clearly structured presentations on familiar subjects (B1+), 3. understand announcements and messages on concrete topics in standard language at a normal pace (B2), 4. follow a large number of films with a plot mainly conveyed by images and action (B1).	Learners can understand straightforward factual information on common everyday- or work related topics and recognise the main themes and individual information if spoken in clear standard speech (B1+).	All students obtaining a *Mittlerer Abschluss*.

Note. HSA – Hauptschulabschluss, MSA – Mittlerer Schulabschluss.

Table C6
Types of Writing Competencies in the NES

	The learners can …	The learners can write a series of simple sentences about their own family, their personal circumstances and their school. They can give a very short, basic description of events, activities, plans and personal experiences plus write short stories following language guidelines (A2/A2+).	All students obtaining a *Hauptschulabschluss*.
NES – HSA (2004)	1. write short, simple notes and reports referring to immediate needs and necessities (A2), 2. write simple personal letters and e-mails (A2), 3. write short simple texts (reports, descriptions, stories, poems) following language guidelines (A2).		
NES – MA (2003)	*The learners can …* 1. take notes if somebody asks for information or explains a problem (B1+), 2. convey messages, simple information and thoughts in personal letters (B1), 3. phrase simple targeted standardised letters and e-mails, for example enquiries, applications (B1), 4. write uncomplicated, detailed texts on a number of different topics on their areas of interest, for example reports, stories, descriptions (B1), 5. write short simple essays on topics of general interest (B1), 6. write short reports on familiar topics, use them to pass on information, provide reasons for action and comment (B 1+).	The learners can write coherent texts on familiar topics of interest (B1).	All students obtaining a *Mittlerer Abschluss*.

Note. HSA – Hauptschulabschluss, MSA – Mittlerer Schulabschluss.

Appendix D:
Rating Scales for Writing Tasks

Table D1

Rating Scale for Level A1

Task fulfilment [TF]	1. Most of the expected content points [80%] are mentioned. 2. Most of the ideas [80%] are relevant to the task. 3. Register and tone are appropriate for the target audience; the simplest everyday polite forms are shown [if applicable]. 4. Meets text type requirements [i. e., following standard format; if applicable]. 5. Communicative effect mainly achieved, i. e., the message is mainly [80%] conveyed although some difficulty is likely to be experienced by the reader.
Organisation [O] [if applicable]	Can link words or groups of words with very basic linear connectors like 'and' or 'then'. Apart from that, words/groups of words are not connected by cohesive ties.
Grammar [G] [if applicable] Accuracy has to be treated in relation to range.	**Range** 1. Shows only a few simple grammatical structures (such as simple present tense, simple modals) and phrase / sentence patterns (such as simple noun + verb phrases, simple sentences / SPO) in a learnt repertoire. **Accuracy** 2. Forms simple phrases (syntax) correctly. *Any structures beyond the targeted level are likely to be used inaccurately which may hinder understanding.* *Performance may show serious mother tongue influences.*
Vocabulary [V] Accuracy has to be treated in relation to range.	**Range** 1. Shows an elementary vocabulary[1] range of isolated words and phrases restricted to particular concrete situations. **Accuracy** 2. Shows control of a few elementary words. *Words beyond the targeted level are likely to be used inaccurately / inappropriately.* *Most frequently used words may be correctly spelled, but words beyond that are exposed to spelling errors.* *Performance may show serious mother tongue influences.*

Note. Rating Guidelines in italics.

1 *Elementary* vocab: names, dates, nationality and words that express needs w/n survival situations, surroundings, limited social demands, food, lodging, transport, etc.

Table D2
Rating Scale for Level A2

Task fulfilment [TF]	1. Most of the expected content points [80%] are mentioned. 2. Most of the ideas [80%] are relevant to the task 3. Register and tone are appropriate for the target audience; simple everyday polite forms are shown [if applicable]. 4. Meets text type requirements [i. e., following a standard format, if applicable] 5. Communicative effect mainly achieved i.e. the message is mainly [80%] conveyed although some difficulty may be experienced by the reader.	
Organisation [O] **Structure and cohesion should have EQUAL WEIGHTING**	**Structure / Thematic development** 1. Text shows logical order but there might be "jumpiness" in the thematic development *or* the thematic development might be illogical in some parts. The end might be missing. *Tells a story or describes something in a simple list of points (uses task bullets to structure text).* *Text not usually organised in paragraphs.* **Language / Cohesion** 2. Links a series of simple phrases / sentences / groups of words using simple cohesive devices, such as articles, pronouns and connectors (the most frequent ones like 'and', 'but', 'because', 'so', 'then', 'after'). *Cohesive devices are not yet found throughout the text; their limited control may sometimes impede communication.*	
Grammar [G] **Accuracy has to be treated in relation to range.**	**Range** 1. Uses some simple structures (such as present/past/future; simple modals, e.g., 'can/may/must'; auxiliaries, e. g. 'to be/have') and some simple sentence patterns (e.g., questions/answers, negatives/positives, commands, suggestions). **Accuracy** 2. Shows control of a few simple structures and patterns. 3. Local errors[2] *may* occur frequently (i.e. in nearly every sentence). 4. Some global errors[3] *are likely to* occur. *Performance may show noticeable mother tongue influence.*	
Vocabulary [V] **Accuracy has to be treated in relation to range.**	**Range** 1. Has a basic range of vocabulary but is able to express basic communicative needs. **Accuracy** 2. Shows control [i.e. adequate and appropriate use] of elementary[1] vocabulary. 3. Non-impeding[4] errors *may* occur frequently. 4. Some impeding[5] errors *may* occur. *Spelling errors may often occur.* *Performance may show noticeable mother tongue influence.*	

Note. Rating Guidelines in italics.

1 *Elementary* vocab: names, dates, nationality and words that express needs w/n survival situations, surroundings, limited social demands, food, lodging, transport, etc.
2 *Local errors* are grammatical errors within one sentence which do not hinder understanding [e.g., mixing up of tenses, forgetting to mark agreement, problems with subordinate clauses, errors in word order]. It is usually clear what the writer wants to express.
3 *Global errors* are those grammatical errors which hinder understanding at the sentence level.
4 *Non-impeding errors* are those lexical / spelling errors which can be resolved spontaneously.
5 *Impeding errors* are those lexical / spelling errors which are irresolvable or take a great deal of effort to resolve.

Table D3
Rating Scale for Level B1

Task fulfilment [TF]	1. Most of the expected content points [80%] are mentioned *or* some content points are dealt with in more depth while others are missing *or* all content points are addressed shortly 2. Most of the ideas [80%] are relevant to the task 3. Register and tone are consistent and appropriate for the target audience. 4. Meets text type requirements [i. e., following a standard / conventional format, if not already provided as part of the task]. 5. Communicative effect is mainly achieved [i. e., the message is mainly [80%] conveyed although occasional difficulty may be experienced by the reader.	
Organisation [O] **Structure and cohesion should have EQUAL WEIGHTING**	**Structure / Thematic development** 1. Produces a straightforward connected piece of text (narrative or description) in a reasonably fluent manner, *or* links a series of shorter discrete simple elements into a linear sequence of points in a reasonably fluent manner. Thematic development shows a logical order and is rounded off. *Longer texts might compensate for some jumpiness or a missing ending.* *Organisation in paragraphs not required, but might compensate for flaws in thematic development.* **Language / Cohesion** 2. Uses a number of common cohesive devices throughout the text, such as articles, pronouns, semantic fields, connectors, discourse markers (like 'so' (consecutive), 'in my opinion'). 3. Shows reasonable control of common cohesive devices. *The use of more elaborate cohesive devices may sometimes impede communication.*	
Grammar [G] **Accuracy has to be treated in relation to range.**	**Range** 1. Uses a range of frequently used structures (such as tenses, simple passives, modals, comparisons, complementation, adverbials, quantifiers, numerals, adverbs). 2. Sentence patterns show simple variations (e. g. subordinate and coordinate clauses often beginning with 'when', 'but'; relative clauses and if-clauses). **Accuracy** 3. Structures and sentence patterns shown in the script are used reasonably accurately. 4. Some local errors[2] occur, but it is clear what he/she is trying to express. 5. Few global errors[3] *may* occur, especially when using more complex structures / sentence patterns (e. g. relative clauses, if-clauses, passives and indirect speech). *Occasionally mother tongue influence may be noticeable.*	

Vocabulary [V] **Accuracy has to be treated in relation to range.**	**Range** 1. Shows a sufficient range of vocabulary [beyond basic] to express him/herself in familiar situations; some circumlocutions may occur in unfamiliar situations. **Accuracy** 2. Shows good control (i.e. adequate and appropriate use) of basic vocabulary. 3. Some non-impeding[4] errors occur. 4. Impeding[5] errors *may* occur occasionally, especially when expressing more complex thoughts or handling unfamiliar topics and situations. *Errors may occur in the field of collocations and complementation.* *Some spelling errors may occur.* *Occasionally mother tongue influence may be noticeable.*

Note. Rating Guidelines in italics.

2 *Local errors* are grammatical errors within one sentence which do not hinder understanding [e.g., mixing up of tenses, forgetting to mark agreement, problems with subordinate clauses, errors in word order]. It is usually clear what the writer wants to express.

3 *Global errors* are those grammatical errors which hinder understanding at the sentence level.

4 *Non-impeding errors* are those lexical / spelling errors which can be resolved spontaneously.

5 *Impeding errors* are those lexical / spelling errors which are irresolvable or take a great deal of effort to resolve.

Table D4
Rating Scale for Level B2

Task Fulfilment [TF]	1. All expected content points are mentioned, but not necessarily in great detail *or* some content point(s) are addressed in an elaborate way / in detail (without relevant aspects missing). 2. Nearly all of the ideas [90%] are relevant to the task 3. Register and tone are consistent and appropriate for the target audience, i.e. in terms of formal and informal register to the situation and persons concerned. 4. Meets text type requirements [i. e., following a standard format]. 5. Communicative effect is achieved. The performance is understandable. Little difficulty is experienced by the reader.
Organisation [O] **Structure and cohesion should have EQUAL WEIGHTING**	**Structure / Thematic development** 1. Organisation of content elements is logical and macrostructure is on the whole clearly developed, although there may be some 'jumpiness' in a long text. 2. Develops a clear, detailed text, expanding and supporting his/her main points with relevant supporting details and examples [microstructure] *or* synthesises and evaluates information and arguments from a number of sources [if applicable]. 3. Text is organised in paragraphs. *Appropriate thematic development might compensate for missing paragraphs.* **Language / Cohesion** 4. Uses a range of common and elaborate cohesive devices [like using pronouns/ articles for complex referencing; 'on the one hand – on the other hand'; 'nevertheless', 'however', 'and this means', 'the most important thing is', 'what I'd prefer is'] efficiently to mark clearly the relationships between ideas and to link utterances into clear, coherent text. *Errors in the field of cohesive devices may occur occasionally but do not impede understanding.*
Grammar [G] **Accuracy has to be treated in relation to range.**	**Range** 1. Uses a good range of frequent and also infrequent structures and some complex sentence patterns in order to give clear descriptions, express viewpoints on most general topics. *More complex forms are not always used in a natural way.* **Accuracy** 2. Shows good grammatical control. 3. Occasional 'slips' or non-systematic errors and minor flaws in sentence structure *may* still occur, but they are rare and do not lead to misunderstanding. 4. Performance is practically free of global errors[3].

Vocabulary [V] Accuracy has to be treated in relation to range.	**Range** 1. Has a good range of vocabulary for matters connected to his/her field and most general topics. *Varies formulation to avoid frequent repetition, lexical gaps can result in circumlocution.* 2. Shows the most usual collocations and complementations[6]. *The use of idiomatic expressions[7] is not always natural.* **Accuracy** 3. Lexical accuracy (i.e. adequate and appropriate use in accordance with the expected level) is generally high. 4. Non-impeding errors *may* occur, but they are rare.

Note. Rating Guidelines in italics.

3 *Global errors* are those grammatical errors which hinder understanding at the sentence level.

6 The term *collocation* refers to two (or more) words typically being used together (marking idiomatic language use), e .g. "a handsome young guy". Wikipedia states: An arrangement or juxtaposition of words or other elements, especially those that commonly co-occur, such as "bread and butter", "bosom buddy", or "dead serious".

Complementations are those elements an adverb or verb requires in order to take on specific meaning; complementations could be prepositions or a certain form of a verb, e. g. compare the meaning of "to stop" in "He stopped smoking" as compared to "He stopped to smoke".

7 *Idiomatic expressions* are groups of words, phrases or expressions that mark natural, typical language use. The vocabulary of a language allows for many combinations of words to form expressions, but only a few are actually used by native speakers. This natural, typical way of expressing something is called *idiomatic language use*.

Table D5
Rating Scale for Level C1

Task Fulfilment [TF]	1. All expected content points are addressed in an elaborate way *or* those points addressed are of such quality that the task content is satisfactorily addressed. 2. All of the ideas are relevant to the task. 3. Register and tone are consistent and appropriate for the target audience, i.e. formal and informal register, appropriate to situation and persons concerned, including emotional, allusive and joking usage. 4. Meets text type requirements [i. e., following a standard format]. 5. Communicative effect is achieved. Expresses him/herself in such a way that the writing intention is completely understandable. Relates to reader in a flexible and efficient way. No difficulty is experienced by the reader.	
Organisation [O] **Structure and cohesion should have EQUAL WEIGHTING**	**Structure / Thematic development** 1. Writes clear, well-structured texts (e.g., appropriate paragraphing) of complex subjects; introduction leads reader to the point; text is rounded off with an appropriate conclusion. 2. Produces a detailed piece of writing, integrating sub-themes, developing particular aspects, expanding and supporting points of view at some length with sufficient logical reasons and relevant examples. **Language / Cohesion** 3. On the whole, performance shows consistent and continuous controlled use of a repertoire of cohesive devices (e. g. referencing, semantic fields, connectors) which contribute to the coherence of the text.	
Grammar [G] Accuracy has to be treated in relation to range.	**Range** 1. Shows a broad repertoire of linguistic structures allowing him/her to select a formulation to express him/herself clearly in an appropriate style without having to restrict what he/she wants to say. *The flexibility in style and tone may be somewhat limited.* **Accuracy** 2. Consistently maintains a high degree of grammatical accuracy (including complex structures). *Errors are rare and difficult to spot.*	
Vocabulary [V] Accuracy has to be treated in relation to range.	**Range** 1. Shows a broad lexical repertoire allowing gaps to be readily overcome with some circumlocutions. **Accuracy** 2. Has a good command of idiomatic expressions and collocations. 3. Occasional minor slips but no significant vocabulary errors occur.	

Appendix E:
Information on Item Development

Table E1
Timeline of Item Development Process

Year	Month	Activity	Primary Outcomes
2005	August	Preliminary Expert Meeting	Planning of workshop sequence and item development strategy
	September	Expert Meeting I	Discussion and refinement of item development and overall testing strategy
	October	Training Workshop I	Familiarization of item writers with CEF, NES, and Dutch grid; development of test specifications for reading, development of sample reading items
	December	Expert Meeting II	Discussion of criteria for item classification and review; discussion of strategies for standard-setting and linking of test with CEF
2006	January	Training Workshop II	Refinement of items and test specifications for reading; preparation of pre-trial I (reading); familiarization with IQB platform
	March	Training Workshop III	Analysis of results from pre-trial I (reading); development of test specifications for listening; preparation of pre-trial II (reading); development of sample listening items
	April	Expert Meeting III	Refinement of criteria for item classification and review; refinement of strategies for standard-setting and linking of test with CEF
	May	Training Workshop IV	Analysis of results from pre-trial II (reading); refinement of test specifications for listening; review of listening items
	July	Release of RFP for Standard-setting	Release of a request-for-proposal (RFP) for standard-setting services to several international experts and institutions
	September	Training Workshop V	Analysis of results from pre-trial I (listening); development of test specifications for writing; development of sample writing prompts
	October	Deadline for Standard-setting Proposals	Deadline of receipt for proposals for standard-setting services; review of proposals
	October	Expert Meeting III	Review of results from pre-trial II (reading); review of results from extra trial I (reading); discussion of standard-setting strategies based on proposal evaluations; development of strategy for writing
	November	Training Workshop VI	Review of results from pre-trial II (listening); refinement of test specifications for writing; refinement and development of sample writing tasks; development of rating scales
	December	Release of MCP for Standard-setting	Release of a modified cost proposal (MCP) for standard setting services to competing institutions

Year	Month	Activity	Primary Outcomes
2007	January	Deadline for MCP	Deadline for receipt of the MCPs; review of MCPs
		Training Workshop VII	Refinement of test specifications for writing; review of writing tasks; development of writing tasks; planning of pre-trial I (writing)
	March	Expert Meeting IV	Discussion of writing assessment strategy; review of timeline and logistics of field trial; discussion of standard-setting strategy
	April	Training Workshop VIII	Refinement of rating scales for writing; review of writing tasks; review of results from extra trials (reading and listening); development of test specifications for speaking; development of sample speaking tasks; development of rating scales for speaking
	June	Training Workshop IX	Review of empirical results from pre-trial 1 (speaking), review of test specifications for speaking, review of task instructions for speaking, development of item writing guidelines for speaking, review of speaking tasks
	August	Release of Technical Report I	Release of technical report I that covers everything up to the field trial

Table E2
Schedules of Item-writing Workshops

#	Year	Dates	Foci	Schedule	Time (hrs.)
1	2005	October 24–28	Overview Reading	Overview of the project	1
				Familiarization with CEF, NES, Dutch Grid	4
				Development of test specifications for reading	6
				Text-mapping activities for reading	6
				Development of sample reading tasks	12
2	2006	January 9–13	Reading	Review of test specifications for reading	8
				Review of first set of reading items	10
				Development of materials for pre-trial 1 (reading)	6
				Familiarization with IQB platform	3
3	2006	March 20–24	Reading Listening	Review of empirical results from pre-trial 1 (reading)	9
				Discussion of pre-trial implications for the development of further reading items	1.5
				Development of test specifications for listening	7.5
				Development of sample listening tasks	8
				Development of materials for pre-trial 2 (reading)	1
4	2006	May 22–26	Reading Listening	Review of empirical results from pre-trial 2 (reading)	9
				Discussion of pre-trial implications for the development of further reading items	1.5
				Review of test specifications for listening	7.5
				Review of first set of listening items	10.5
5	2006	September 4–8	Listening Writing	Review of empirical results from pre-trial 1 (listening)	9
				Discussion of pre-trial implications for the development of further listening items	1.5
				Overview of writing assessment	3
				Development of test specifications for writing	6
				Development of sample writing tasks	9

#	Year	Dates	Foci	Schedule	Time (hrs.)
6	2006	November 27–December 1	Listening Writing	Review of empirical results from pre-trial 2 (listening)	7
				Review of test specifications for listening	1.5
				Review and development of sample writing tasks	6
				Development of rating scales	6
				Review of test specifications for writing	7.5
7	2007	January 9–13	Writing	Review of test specifications for writing	6
				Review of task instructions for writing	3
				Development of item writing guidelines	3
				Review of writing tasks	9
				Planning of pre-trial I (writing)	6
8	2007	April 20–24	Writing Speaking	Review of empirical results from extra trials (reading and listening)	1.5
				Review of writing tasks and rating scales	1.5
				Development of test specifications for speaking	3
				Development of sample speaking tasks	9
				Review of sample speaking tasks	6
				Development of rating scales	4.5
				Planning of pre-trial II (writing)	4.5
9	2007	June 25–29	Speaking	Feedback from pre-trial 1 (speaking)	1
				Review of rating scales	3
				Interlocutor / rater training	9
				Review of test specifications for speaking	3
				Review of speaking tasks	6
				Review of EALTA and Language Testers' Association	3
				Planning of future item development	1.5

Total Hours of Training Time   253

Table E3

Composition of Student Samples in Pre-trials for Reading and Listening Comprehension as well as Writing

Pre-trial	Booklet #	# of Texts	# of Items	Grade		School Type				Region			
				9	10	HS	RS	GS	GY	North	South	East	West
Reading 1	Overall	20	122	169	155	79	82	28	133	36	118	86	84
	1	5	31	42	40	20	20	8	34	9	30	22	21
	2	5	27	46	35	20	21	7	33	9	31	20	21
	3	5	29	41	40	20	22	7	32	9	29	22	21
	4	5	35	40	40	19	21	6	34	9	28	22	21
Reading 2	Overall	20	139	233	183	100	139	43	134	82	102	89	145
	1	5	36	60	45	28	32	11	34	21	26	21	37
	2	5	31	61	47	28	32	11	37	23	27	21	37
	3	5	36	59	44	22	38	11	32	19	26	23	36
	4	5	36	53	47	22	37	10	31	19	23	24	35
Listening 1	Overall	16	96	320	245	112	166	0	287	58	161	131	215
	1	4	25	115	85	27	59	0	114	6	90	48	56
	2	4	25	65	21	27	36	0	23	26	12	34	14
	3	4	24	85	72	39	41	0	77	19	14	42	82
	4	4	22	55	67	19	30	0	73	7	45	7	63
Listening 2	Overall	20	104	296	234	144	196	79	111	n/a	n/a	n/a	n/a
	1	5	26	48	82	28	59	12	31	n/a	n/a	n/a	n/a
	2	5	25	35	87	27	59	13	23	n/a	n/a	n/a	n/a
	3	5	27	88	44	42	15	54	21	n/a	n/a	n/a	n/a
	4	5	26	125	21	47	63	0	36	n/a	n/a	n/a	n/a
Writing	Overall	20	---	209	256	113	156	88	107	n/a	n/a	n/a	n/a

Note. The information about the geographical composition of students in listening trial 2 and the writing trial was not available at the time of publication of this report.

Table E4

Statistics from Pre-trials Reading and Listening Comprehension

Pre-trial #	Booklet #	# of Texts	# of Items	Booklet Statistics					
				Min	Max	Mean	Cronbach's α	p-bs < .25	p-bs < 0
Reading 1	Overall	20	122						
	1	5	31	7	30	20.8	.82	10	5
	2	5	27	4	27	18.8	.87	5	5
	3	5	29	2	29	21.9	.88	5	5
	4	5	35	11	33	23.7	.76	14	4
Reading 2	Overall	20	139						
	1	5	36	10	34	23.2	.82	12	6
	2	5	31	5	31	20.3	.81	10	5
	3	5	36	4	36	22.7	.90	3	1
	4	5	36	9	35	24.8	.84	8	5
Listening 1	Overall	16	96						
	1	4	25	1	24	10.9	.87	2	2
	2	4	25	1	23	12.1	.84	7	2
	3	4	24	1	21	10.9	.78	7	1
	4	4	22	4	22	12.1	.77	6	2
Listening 2	Overall	20	104						
	1	5	26	0	25	11.7	.90	0	0
	2	5	25	0	19	9.47	.76	8	3
	3	5	27	0	26	8.85	.88	1	1
	4	5	26	1	21	12.9	.79	10	4

Notes. p-bs = point-biserial correlation representing item discrimination. Min = minimum total score. Max = maximum total score.

Appendix F:
Dutch Grid Classification Criteria
for Reading and Listening Tasks

Classification Criteria for Reading Comprehension Items

Text Characteristics

1. Likely to be comprehensible by learner at level … (*A1, A2, B1, B2, C1*)
2. Text type (*timetables, programs, menus, blurbs, instructions, manuals, newspaper articles, magazine articles, leaflets, programs, blurbs, CD covers, reviews, adverts, e-mails, text messages (SMS), personal letters, professional letters, postcards, lyrics, folk stories, literature excerpt, short stories, folk stories, interviews, memos, reports, other*)
3. Text source (*specify*)
4. Domain (*public, personal, occupational, educational, other*)
5. Discourse type (*narrative, descriptive, instructive, expository, argumentative, phatic*)
6. Topic area (*personal identification, house and home, environment, daily life, free time, entertainment media, sports, travel, relations with other people, health and body care, education, shopping, food and drink, services, places, languages, weather, work, multicultural society, crime, global problems, other*)
7. Original target audience for text (*specify*)
8. Authenticity (*authentic, abridged, simplified, glossed*)
9. Structural characteristics of text
    a. Syntax (*only simple, mainly simple, limited range of complex structures, wide range of complex structures*)
    b. Vocabulary (*only frequent, mostly frequent, rather extended, extended*)
    c. Nature of content (*only concrete, mostly concrete, fairly abstract, mainly abstract*)
    d. Text length (*number of words*)
10. Form of text (*prose, pictures, bullets, graphs, tables, captions, other*)
11. Number of items per text (*specify*)

Item Characteristics

1. Likely to be solvable by learner at level … (*A1, A2, B1, B2, C1*)
2. Purpose of reading (*understand the overall idea, understand the main ideas, understand the main ideas with line of argument and supporting details, scan longer texts to locate information, identify specific information, collate information from different texts or part of text, deduce the meaning of unknown words from context, make simple inferences, make complex inferences*)
3. Item type (*multiple choice, true-false-not given, multiple matching, sequencing, gap-filling, short-answer, table completion, sentence completion*)

Classification Criteria for Listening Comprehension Items

Text Characteristics

1. Likely to be comprehensible by learner at level … (*A1, A2, B1, B2, C1*)
2. Input type (*interviews, conversations, dialogues phone conversations, advertisements / commercials, reports, announcements, news, directions, instructions, messages, weather forecasts, stories, songs, lectures, talks, directions, jokes, anecdotes, radio programmes, other*)
3. Input source (*specify*)
4. Domain (*public, personal, occupational, educational, other*)
5. Discourse type (*narrative, descriptive, instructive, expository, argumentative, phatic*)
6. Topic area (*personal identification, house and home, environment, daily life, free time, entertainment media, sports, travel, relations with other people, health and body care, education, shopping, food and drink, services, places, languages, weather, work, multicultural society, crime, global problems, science, other*)
7. Original target audience for input *(specify)*
8. Authenticity
   a. Script (*scripted, semi-scripted, non-scripted*)
   b. Redundancy (*low, medium, high*)
   c. Background Noise (*supporting, disturbing*)
   d. Number of times heard (*once, twice*)
9. Structural characteristics of input
   a. Syntax (*only simple, mainly simple, limited range of complex structures, wide range of complex structures*)
   b. Vocabulary (*only frequent, mostly frequent, rather extended, extended*)
   c. Nature of content (*only concrete, mostly concrete, fairly abstract, mainly abstract*)
   d. Length of input (*number of words, time*)
10. Speaker Characteristics
    a. Number of voices (*one, two, many*)
    b. Accents (*British, American, Australian, other*)
    c. Ethnic background (*native speakers, non-native speakers*)
    d. Gender (*male, female*)
    e. Age (*children, teenagers, adults*)
    f. Speed of articulation (*slow, normal, quick*)
11. Number of items per input (*specify*)

Item Characteristics

12. Likely to be solvable by learner at level … (*A1, A2, B1, B2, C1*)
13. Purpose of listening (*understand the overall idea, understand the main ideas, identify specific information, collate information from different texts or part of text, deduce the meaning of unknown words from context, understand detailed directions, make simple inferences, make complex inferences*)
14. Item type (*multiple choice, table completion, short answer, multiple matching, note-taking*)

Appendix G:
Standardized Feedback Questionnaires for Pre-trials

Reading Test – Feedback Questionnaire
(English Translation of German Original for Technical Report)

Answer questions 1-8 by putting a circle around **one** of the numbers in each row.

1 How <u>familiar</u> did you find the <u>topics</u> of the reading texts?

	Please mark only one box per row!		Not familiar	Not very familiar	Quite familiar	Very familiar
1.1	[text titles to be added here]		①	②	③	④
1.2	↓	↓	①	②	③	④
1.3	↓	↓	①	②	③	④
1.4	↓	↓	①	②	③	④
1.5	↓	↓	①	②	③	④

2 How <u>interesting</u> did you find the texts?

	Please mark only one box per row!		Not interesting	Not very interesting	Quite interesting	Very interesting
2.1	[text titles to be added here]		①	②	③	④
2.2	↓	↓	①	②	③	④
2.3	↓	↓	①	②	③	④
2.4	↓	↓	①	②	③	④
2.5	↓	↓	①	②	③	④

3 How <u>difficult</u> did you find the texts?

	Please mark only one box per row!		Not difficult	Not very difficult	Quite difficult	Very difficult
3.1	[text titles to be added here]		①	②	③	④
3.2	↓	↓	①	②	③	④
3.3	↓	↓	①	②	③	④
3.4	↓	↓	①	②	③	④
3.5	↓	↓	①	②	③	④

4 How <u>familiar</u> were you with the <u>test methods</u> used in this reading test?

	Please mark only one box per row!		Not familiar	Not very familiar	Quite familiar	Very familiar
4.1	[test methods to be added here]		①	②	③	④
4.2	↓	↓	①	②	③	④
4.3	↓	↓	①	②	③	④
4.4	↓	↓	①	②	③	④
4.5	↓	↓	①	②	③	④

5 How <u>suitable</u> did you find the following?

Please mark only one box per row!	Too short	A little too short	Just fine	A little long	Too long
5.1	Length of the reading texts	①	②	③	④	⑤
5.2	Length of the test as a whole	①	②	③	④	⑤
5.3	Amount of time provided	①	②	③	④	⑤

6 How <u>satisfied</u> were you with the following?

Please mark only one box per row!	Not satisfied	Not very satisfied	Quite satisfied	Very satisfied
6.1	Number of words for each answer	①	②	③	④
6.2	Test booklet layout	①	②	③	④
6.3	Instructions in the test	①	②	③	④

7 How well do you feel the test measured your English reading ability?

Very poorly	Poorly	Well	Very well
①	②	③	④

8 Do you feel there are any ways in which you think this test could be improved?

_____

_____

9 Do you have any other comments you would like to make on this reading test?

_____

_____

Thank you!

Listening Test – Feedback Questionnaire
(English Translation of German Original for Technical Report)

0   ID Number _____

On this page and on the back you will find a series of questions about the test that you have just completed. There are no 'correct' or 'incorrect' answers – just your answers. We are interested in your honest opinion about this test!

Please answer the following questions 1-7 by **checking in each line the box that most closely resembles how you feel**. For example, if you were 'not familiar at all' with the topic of a listening passage, then check the leftmost box with the number '1' in it. Questions 8 and 9 are open ended as we are interested in your suggestions for improving the test.

1   How <u>familiar</u> were you with the topic / theme of each listening passage?

	Please mark only one box per row!	Completely unfamiliar	Rather un-familiar	Rather familiar	Very familiar
1.1	[text titles to be added here]	[1]	[2]	[3]	[4]
1.2	[text titles to be added here]	[1]	[2]	[3]	[4]
1.3	[text titles to be added here]	[1]	[2]	[3]	[4]
1.4	[text titles to be added here]	[1]	[2]	[3]	[4]

2   How <u>interesting</u> did you find the texts?

	Please mark only one box per row!	Not interesting	Rather uninteresting	Rather interesting	Very interesting
2.1	[text titles to be added here]	[1]	[2]	[3]	[4]
2.2	[text titles to be added here]	[1]	[2]	[3]	[4]
2.3	[text titles to be added here]	[1]	[2]	[3]	[4]
2.4	[text titles to be added here]	[1]	[2]	[3]	[4]

3   How <u>difficult</u> did you find the texts?

	Please mark only one box per row!	Not difficult	Rather easy	Somewhat difficult	Very difficult
3.1	[text titles to be added here]	[1]	[2]	[3]	[4]
3.2	[text titles to be added here]	[1]	[2]	[3]	[4]
3.3	[text titles to be added here]	[1]	[2]	[3]	[4]
3.4	[text titles to be added here]	[1]	[2]	[3]	[4]

4   How <u>familiar</u> were you with the different <u>question types</u>?

	Please mark only one box per row!	Not familiar	Rather unfamiliar	Rather familiar	Very familiar
4.1	Multiple-choice answers	[1]	[2]	[3]	[4]
4.2	Short answers	[1]	[2]	[3]	[4]
4.3	Completing tables	[1]	[2]	[3]	[4]
4.4	Multiple matching	[1]	[2]	[3]	[4]

5 How did you find the <u>time allotments</u> for different tasks?

	Please mark only one box per row!	Much too short	A bit too short	Just right	A bit too long	Much too long
5.1	Time to read the questions	1	2	3	4	5
5.2	Time to answer the questions	1	2	3	4	5
5.3	**Length of the individual passages:**					
	[text titles to be added here]	1	2	3	4	5
	[text titles to be added here]	1	2	3	4	5
	[text titles to be added here]	1	2	3	4	5
	[text titles to be added here]	1	2	3	4	5
5.4	Length of the passages overall	1	2	3	4	5

6 How <u>satisfied</u> were you with the following aspects of the test?

	Please mark only one box per row!	Dissatisfied	Rather dissatisfied	Rather satisfied	Satisfied
6.1	**Number of speakers:**				
	[text titles to be added here]	1	2	3	4
	[text titles to be added here]	1	2	3	4
	[text titles to be added here]	1	2	3	4
	[text titles to be added here]	1	2	3	4
6.2	**Number of speakers on the tape:**				
	[text titles to be added here]	1	2	3	4
	[text titles to be added here]	1	2	3	4
	[text titles to be added here]	1	2	3	4
	[text titles to be added here]	1	2	3	4
6.3	**Rate of speech:**				
	[text titles to be added here]	1	2	3	4
	[text titles to be added here]	1	2	3	4
	[text titles to be added here]	1	2	3	4
	[text titles to be added here]	1	2	3	4
6.4	Clarity of Instructions	1	2	3	4
6.5	Quality of the recordings	1	2	3	4
6.6	Restriction on the number of words required to answer questions	1	2	3	4
6.7	Layout of the test	1	2	3	4

7 How well do you feel the test measured your English listening ability?

Very poorly	Poorly	Well	Very well
1	2	3	4

8 Do you feel there are any ways in which you think this test could be improved?

_____

_____

9 Do you have any other comments you would like to make on this reading test?

_____

Writing Test — Feedback Questionnaire
(English Translation of German Original for Technical Report)

0 ID Number _____

On this page and on the back you will find a series of questions about the test that you have just completed. There are no 'correct' or 'incorrect' answers – just your answers. We are interested in your honest opinion about this test!

Please answer the following questions 1-8 by **checking in each line the box that most closely resembles how you feel**. For example, if you were 'not familiar at all' with the topic of a writing task passage, then check the leftmost box with the number '1' in it. Questions 7 and 8 are open ended as we are interested in your suggestions for improving the test.

1 How **familiar** were you with the **themes / topics** of the writing tasks?

	Please mark only one box per row!	Completely unfamiliar	Rather unfamiliar	Rather familiar	Very familiar
1.1	[task titles to be added here]	[1]	[2]	[3]	[4]
1.2		[1]	[2]	[3]	[4]
1.3		[1]	[2]	[3]	[4]

2 How **interesting** did you find the writing tasks?

	Please mark only one box per row!	Not interesting	Rather uninteresting	Rather interesting	Very interesting
2.1	[task titles to be added here]	[1]	[2]	[3]	[4]
2.2		[1]	[2]	[3]	[4]
2.3		[1]	[2]	[3]	[4]

3 How **difficult** did you find the writing tasks?

	Please mark only one box per row!	Not difficult at all	Not very difficult	Somewhat difficult	Very difficult
3.1	[task titles to be added here]	[1]	[2]	[3]	[4]
3.2		[1]	[2]	[3]	[4]
3.3		[1]	[2]	[3]	[4]

4 How **familiar** were you with the **different types** of writing task?

	Please mark only one box per row!	Not familiar	Rather unfamliar	Somewhat familiar	Very familiar
4.1	[task titles to be added here]	[1]	[2]	[3]	[4]
4.2		[1]	[2]	[3]	[4]
4.3		[1]	[2]	[3]	[4]

5 How <u>satisfied</u> were you with the following <u>aspects</u> of the writing tasks?

	Please mark only one box per row!	Unsuitable	Somewhat unsuitable	Suitable	Very suitable
5.1	Clarity of instructions	①	②	③	④
5.2	Length of expected answer [# words]	①	②	③	④
5.3	Layout / design of test booklet	①	②	③	④
5.4	Pictures	①	②	③	④
5.5	Space for responding	①	②	③	④
5.6.1	Time for task 1 [25 minutes]	①	②	③	④
5.6.2	Time for task 2 [35 minutes]	①	②	③	④
5.6.3	Time for task 3 [45 minutes]	①	②	③	④
5.7	Time for all tasks	①	②	③	④

6 How <u>well</u> did the test measure your <u>writing ability</u> in English?

Please mark only one box!

Very poorly	Rather poorly	Rather well	Very well
①	②	③	④

7 How could this writing test be improved?

_____
_____
_____
_____
_____

8 Do you have any additional remarks on this writing test?!

_____
_____
_____
_____
_____

Thank you!

Authors

André A. Rupp
André A. Rupp is an Assistant Professor in the Department of Measurement, Statistics, and Evaluation (EDMS) at the University of Maryland in the U.S. After completing his graduate work in applied linguistics, statistics, and research methods in the U.S. and Canada, he started his academic career at the bilingual University of Ottawa. Until recently, Dr. Rupp then worked at the Institute for Educational Progress (Institut zur Qualitätsentwicklung im Bildungswesen, IQB) at Humboldt University in Berlin, Germany with his fellow co-authors where he consulted in the project described in this book. His current research interests center around cognitively-grounded assessment approaches and associated statistical models. They include investigating the theoretical potential and practical limitations of such cognitive diagnosis models, developing principled diagnostic assessment approaches for complex skill sets, and researching the impact of large-scale design structures on model fit within such contexts.

Miriam Vock
Miriam Vock is a research scientist at the Institute for Educational Progress (IQB) at Humboldt University in Berlin, Germany. She received her Masters degree in psychology from the University of Münster, Germany, in 2000, where she worked in several scientific projects concerning the development of intelligence tests, program evaluation and research on giftedness and talent. In 2004, she obtained her PhD degree in Psychology from the University of Münster, Germany. In her dissertation, she developed IRT based working memory scales for the assessment of cognitive abilities in children. At the IQB, her research interests focus on the development and validation of standards-based tasks, the psychological factors which influence the academic development of students, and specific developmental trajectories of gifted students.

Claudia Harsch
Claudia Harsch is a research scientist at the Institute for Educational Progress (IQB). She received her Masters degree in Didactics of Foreign Languages and Applied Linguistics in German and English from the University of Augsburg, Germany, in 2001. She then worked at Augsburg University in several language testing projects. Her PhD thesis investigates the relevance of the *Common European Framework of Reference* for various aspects of language assessment. She obtained her PhD degree in 2006. From 2005 on, she consulted the test developer team at the IQB. She has been working at the IQB since 2007, where her research interests focus on the training of item developers, on the development of foreign language tests with special focus on instruments for assessing writing, and on the implementation of the *Common European Framework* in the foreign language classroom.

Olaf Köller
Olaf Köller is director of the Institute for Educational Progress (IQB) and full professor of educational research at Humboldt University, Berlin. After graduating in psychology in 1991, he started his scientific career at the Institute for Science Education (IPN) at the University of Kiel, Germany. In 1996 he moved to the Max Planck Institute for Human Development, where he finished his doctoral dissertation in 1997. In 2002 he accepted a full professorship at the University of Erlangen-Nuremberg, before moving to his current position at Humboldt University in 2004. As director of the IQB, Olaf Köller is responsible for the national assessment program in Germany. Aside from his activities in academic assessment, his major research interests are reciprocal effects of academic self-concepts and achievement, the development of academic interests and their effects on achievement, and educational and occupational choices.